AF599271

THE BIG PICTURE

THE BIG PICTURE

A Personal History of Independent Television Production in Canada

PAT FERNS

TORONTO, 2025

Sutherland House
416 Moore Ave., Suite 304
Toronto, ON M4G 1C9

Copyright © 2025 by Pat Ferns

All rights reserved, including the right to reproduce this book or portions thereof in any form whatsoever. For information on rights and permissions or to request a special discount for bulk purchases, please contact Sutherland House at info@sutherlandhousebooks.com

Sutherland House and logo are registered trademarks of The Sutherland House Inc.

First edition, June 2025

If you are interested in inviting one of our authors to a live event or media appearance, please contact sranasinghe@sutherlandhousebooks.com and visit our website at sutherlandhousebooks.com for more information about our authors and their schedules.

We acknowledge the support of the Government of Canada.

Manufactured in Turkey
Cover designed by Luisa Galstyan and Jordan Lunn

Library and Archives Canada Cataloguing in Publication
Title: The big picture : a personal history of independent television production in Canada / Pat Ferns.
Names: Ferns, Pat, author.
Description: Includes index.
Identifiers: Canadiana (print) 20250131706 | Canadiana (ebook) 20250131714 | ISBN 9781998365630 (hardcover) | ISBN 9781998365647 (EPUB)
Subjects: LCSH: Television broadcasting—Canada—History. | LCSH: Television—Production and direction—Canada—History.
Classification: LCC HE8700.9.C3 F44 2025 | DDC 384.550971—dc23

ISBN 978-1-998365-63-0
eBook 978-1-998365-64-7

CONTENTS

PART THREE: PRIMEDIA

PART FOUR: BANFF

PART FIVE: FERNS PRODUCTIONS

"Those roles which, being neither those of Hero nor Heroine, Confidante or Villain, but which were nonetheless essential to bring about the Recognition or the denouement, were called Fifth Business in drama and opera companies organized according to the old style; the player who acted these parts was often referred to as Fifth Business."

Thomas Overskou, *Den Dansk Skueplads*,
quoted in Robertson Davies' *Fifth Business*

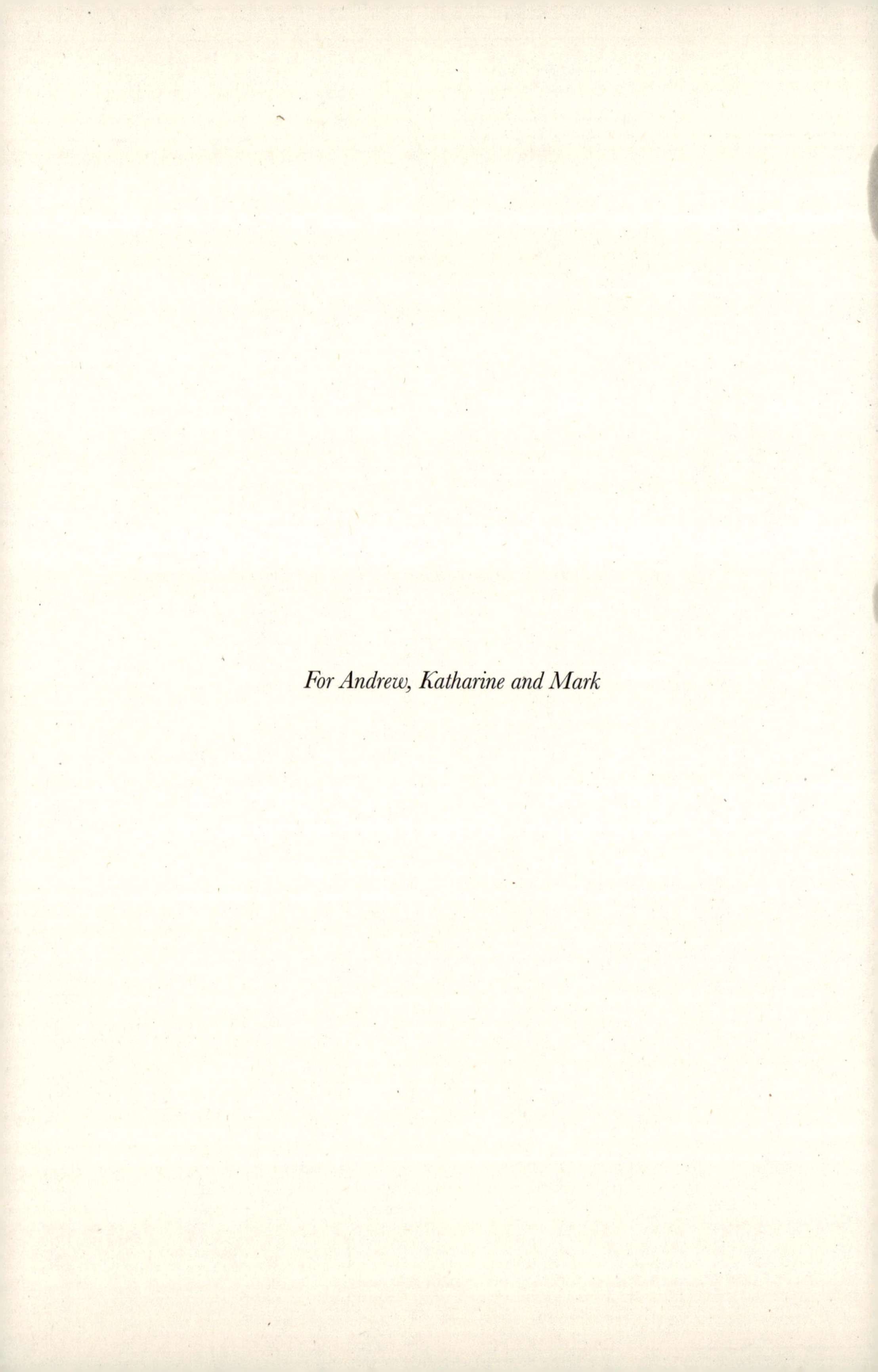

For Andrew, Katharine and Mark

PROLOGUE

"BUT WHAT'S AN AUTOBIOGRAPHY? Surely, it's a romance of which one is oneself the hero." So writes Robertson Davies in *World of Wonders,* the third volume of *The Deptford Trilogy* of which *Fifth Business* is the first, Am I the hero of this story? No. The heroes are a band of entrepreneurs who believed in Canadian talent and sought to put it on a world stage. My role was "Fifth Business"—essential to the plot, but not the protagonist—just a player in a highly collaborative art form. I was there when Canada's "indies" grew from humble beginnings to become, as of 2024, a $12.2 billion production sector generating $14.1 billion in GDP and almost a quarter of a million jobs. I was close to the action, and I can tell the tale: a personal memoir and the story of independent television production in Canada.

As a Canadian, educated in the UK, I returned to my native land in 1968 to join the Canadian Broadcasting Corporation, where I met my mentor and future business partner Richard Nielsen. Together we left the CBC to create a boutique, independent production company that was soon acquired by a media giant in their abortive effort to be granted a broadcast licence. It was during this period of so-called "stability" that I was able to focus my efforts on lobbying for the policies and institutions that were to prove crucial to the building of a viable production industry.

Dick Nielsen and I eventually decided to go our separate ways, with me focusing on developing a business based on international co-production, showcasing Canadian talent to the world. Despite my connection to the UK and Europe, I was a fervent Canadian nationalist. I decided to remain here while others were moving overseas or south of the border. I wanted Canada to be the stage on which to tell Canadian stories with Canadian storytellers.

The year Dick and I parted company, Telefilm Canada's Broadcast Program Development Fund, an idea I had proposed years before, finally came to be. In the 1990s I co-drafted the key principles of the Cable Fund, and I was there with my campaigning colleagues when these two funds were amalgamated into a public/private partnership. Since 2010, this has been known as the Canada Media Fund, and it is the largest arts enterprise in the nation.

In parallel to building my own company, I worked as a volunteer board member and then chair of the Banff Television Foundation, establishing the Banff Television Festival (now the Banff World Media Festival) as one of the world's leading industry events. Eventually I joined its staff, becoming its president and CEO and expanding (some say over-expanding) its scale and impact.

Public pitching, a format I created at Banff to assist Canadian independent producers in Canada, ended up spreading around the globe, and I went with it across five continents, creating, developing, and shaping events from China and Taiwan to Israel and Italy.

After leaving Banff and moving to the West Coast, I re-established myself as a producer and concentrated on creating productions and media events not only in Canada but worldwide.

With its mass audience, television, far more than motion pictures, transformed the independent production industry in Canada. My colleagues and I were there at the heart of that revolution.

The lives we lived were shaped by forces bigger than us. These forces shaped our culture: storytellers and values, government regulation and the market, and perhaps most importantly of all, technology. I began my career in 1968 in an analogue world of black-and-white 16 mm films, negative cutters, and unwieldy two-inch videotapes, and my career ended in a wholly digital world in glorious 4K colour managed from a computer. It's a fascinating, multidimensional story, yet as Olivier Côté, curator of the Canadian Museum of History, has observed: "Television remains, among the Canadian cultural industries, strangely neglected as an object of study."

This book aims to rectify that neglect. It is a "rags to riches" account of an exciting era of cultural and business development. Unfortunately, it is also the story of a five-decade era that has now come to an end. As the industry endures yet another brutal transformation, when "big," "integrated," and "consolidated" are the watchwords as content providers seek to secure their sources of supply, the era of the small independent producer is over. I was there when incentives and regulation built it; technology and the market have killed it. It is no longer possible to pursue the Canadian independent producer's dream. Michael Macmillan, who started his life in film as a student at Queen's University, created Atlantis with a few colleagues, merged with Alliance, was bought out, and the resulting company became e-One, and now an American-owned global entertainment giant. A film student these days, in our era of consolidation, cannot follow in Michael's footsteps, and rather than create a small company, they would be better off positioning themselves as freelance talent and either selling services to, or even joining, one of the giants.

To understand the story I am about to tell, we must first understand Canada's cultural policies since the Second World War, starting with the Royal Commission on National Development in the Arts, Letters and Sciences, better known as the Massey Commission. Founded in 1949, it held a series of public hearings across Canada, and issued a report in 1951 concluding the arts are central to a strong sense of national community, and that the government had a responsibility to provide public funding to encourage work in the arts, humanities, and social sciences. It prioritized more money for universities and a strengthening of public broadcasting. Moreover, the report stated that without such funding, authentic Canadian culture would be crowded out by cheaper American popular culture:

> What, we may ask ourselves, are we defending? We are defending civilization, our share of it, our contribution to it. The things with which our inquiry deals are the elements which give civilization its character and meaning. It would be paradoxical to defend something which we are unwilling to strengthen and enrich, and which we would even allow to decline.

The government accepted Massey's recommendations on university funding and supporting the CBC (Canadian Broadcasting Corporation), but otherwise it largely ignored the rest of the report. However, in time, the report can be credited for the establishment of the National Library of Canada (1953) and the Canada Council for the Encouragement of the Arts, Letters, Humanities, and Social Sciences (1957). In 1967, the government ignored Massey's recommendation not to support a private film industry and created the Canadian Film Development Corporation (CFDC) to subsidize motion pictures.

As ever in matters of cultural policy, Quebec pursued its own path, dismissing the Massey report as an elitist cultural document, reflecting an Anglophone conservative version of culture at the expense of Quebec's historic cultural heritage. La Belle Province was fighting for cultural survival given the dominance of the English language in Canada, whereas English Canada was grappling with the dominance of the United States within North American culture. Both conflicts are unending and we have become all too familiar with their various iterations.

More interesting perhaps is the tension between the values of a free-market economy where profit and monetary gain reign supreme, and the notion of art, which requires patronage: funding to encourage challenge and to subsidize risk, experiment, and criticism. As often in Canada, we sought a middle ground between public support and creative competition, but we have often failed to find the right balance, lurching from favouring one to the other, and beset by bureaucratization. Governments, both Liberal and Conservative, have exhibited ambivalence in the execution of cultural policies, for example in 1992, when the government expanded the responsibilities of the CBC, almost immediately followed by substantial budget cuts.

The question has always been how to create a viable Canadian entertainment industry in the face of changing technology and overwhelming competition from the most successful popular culture the world has ever witnessed. In the case of cinema, Hollywood owned the means of distribution and theatrical exhibition in Canada; and as regards television, America simply dumped its content on Canadian screens. How could Canada maintain its voice against this onslaught? At the beginning of my era, "Canadian content" meant news, weather, and sports, and the only scripted television was produced in-house by the CBC and Radio-Canada. How could talent flourish in such an environment? How would the rich diversity of Canadian stories be told?

What was required was both government regulation and the freedom to compete. These two concepts can co-exist, but it is a very delicate balancing act. When I joined the industry in 1968, quotas were the subject of much discussion. I recognized that Canadian content quotas might work for radio, and even more so for the music business. However, such regulation was consistently subverted in television, and impossible for film. Canada eventually produced a viable and diverse music industry, and our literary talents were already world-class. But in scripted film and television, it would prove much more complex. Screenwriters did not have enough opportunity to write to enable them to improve their skills. And the same was true for technical talent: when I began, the sound on Canadian movies was notoriously bad. I came to see that quality is in part a function of quantity, or more simply put, the opportunity to practice. Lax tax shelter rules created a flood of bad Canadian movies in the 1970s, but even bad movies create work for Canadian crews, and with work came experience, and eventually expertise.

My origins—a Canadian raised abroad—profoundly shaped my perception of Canada. Formative years become the bedrock on which future careers are built. I always wanted to be the best, but fate dictated that my talent was not as a film director or creative writer, but as a producer—"Fifth Business" as it were—and my role was to get the story told, make others look good, and remain in the shadows. In this industry, the producer is the junction point where the creative and the entrepreneurial come together. The producer finds the script, but must also find the money. The producer hires the director, but has the power to fire the director.

Yes, ultimately, power and responsibility reside in the person of the producer. My professional life has been devoted to making a difference. But in order to make a difference **and** to help create a sustainable independent industry, I had to come out of the shadows and be on-stage. I was forced into the spotlight to lead a crusade along with other Canadian independent producers to create a better world for all of us. Fortunately, my ideas and strategies struck a chord with my contemporaries. And it was this group of us acting in concert that made the difference.

When I joined the industry in 1968, broadcast television was clearly in its ascendancy. Three networks in the USA—ABC, CBS, and NBC—shared over ninety percent of the audience. There were two networks in Canada—one public and one private. In the UK a third network had just been added—BBC2—to expand the existing duopoly. The 1960s saw the introduction of colour television. But essentially the technology of television receivers meant that choice was constrained by the dial. It was only in the 1970s that cable television became a possibility: its growth in the USA from less than 10 percent in the 1970s to 23 percent in 1980 rising to over 60 percent by 1990 meant that new services could be added. Thanks to cable and satellite technology, specialty channels developed and, in due course, subscription television. This was transformational. The growth of cable and satellite television eroded the primacy of broadcast networks to curate your television viewing. Viewers wanted more choice and technology delivered. But the real revolution where you could curate your own viewing by choosing what you wanted to watch when you wanted to watch it required the transition from analogue to digital: this came in the first decade of the new century. If pay, subscription, and specialty had stolen the broadcasters' lunch in the 1990s, the technology giants were getting ready to create a feeding frenzy. We now see the media landscape dominated by technology companies: Amazon, Apple, Alphabet (Google), and Microsoft have raced ahead of even Disney and Warner Brothers-Discovery. Where are ABC, CBS, and NBC now?

When I began my journey, the independent production industry was peopled with larger-than-life characters and featured scenes of savage political in-fighting. I was at the centre of the action in Montreal, Toronto, and Ottawa while preaching the gospel of independent production from coast to coast. For me as an evangelist, the main prize was opportunity for Canadians to tell their own stories with sufficient resources and professional skills to avoid unfavourable comparison with American and European content. We had to find our voice.

In this attempt to show how we found that voice, I have drawn on both the public record and my own experiences. While some of my files have been lost along the way, I made sure to keep some form of calendar from the start of my career. I've checked my anecdotes against this chronology, and I was often surprised to find that the time frame was different than I remembered it. I consulted widely with former colleagues, especially those who did the hard work in committees and hearings as we fought for our very existence, to see if they remember the story as I do and to create a more factual and respectful account of the development of this industry. Where necessary, they have corrected my account.

Perhaps Sharon Butala says it best in *The Perfection of the Morning*: "There's a way in which all non-fiction is fiction: the backward search through happenstance, trivia, the flotsam and jetsam of life to search out a pattern, themes, a meaning is by its nature an imposition of order onto what was chaotic."

PART ONE

GROWING UP

CHAPTER 1

ORIGINS AND EXILE (1945–1949)

I WAS BORN IN WINNIPEG, Manitoba, on January 13, 1945, the second son of Harry and Maureen Ferns, and was given the name William Paterson, after my dad's best friend, whose nickname, "Pat," I also inherited. A grandson of one of Wilfred Laurier's ministers, "Pat" Paterson had a great interest in politics and was a committed Canadian nationalist. My father met him when they were both working in Ottawa in the Prime Minister's Office. Bright young men at the centre of Canada's war effort, Pat was a Liberal and my Dad a Marxist, so theirs was a stormy relationship. Neither would yield in their ideological arguments. Though Pat started the war as something of an isolationist, he was increasingly critical of Western European leaders' timid response to Hitler. Pat feared a triumph for the Nazis. But it was not this that led him to quit the PMO. Both he and my Dad worked for Leonard Brockington, a Special Assistant to the Prime Minister. Before the war, Brockington had served as the first

Chairman of the Canadian Broadcasting Corporation, and after the war he became Chairman of Odeon Theatres of Canada.

What caused Pat to leave the PMO in 1941 was a Dominion-Provincial conference designed to change the federal/provincial relationship in the interest of all Canadians: a noble goal. Most of the provincial leaders struck Dad and Pat as unimpressive, with the exception of Manitoba's John Bracken, so they believed Prime Minister Mackenzie King would prevail, as he had the better arguments. Instead, King chose not to fight, but to wind up the conference. Pat was heartbroken. As my father recalled, "The littleness of the men assembled at the conference and their crabbed and mean provincialism was a humiliation to the proud and intelligent man that Pat was."

Brockington did not want to see the war effort lose such a brilliant mind, so he asked his friend William Stephenson (the "Man called Intrepid") to find a position for Pat in the British Office of Information recently established in New York. Pat could better fight the Nazis from there. While at first it was absorbing to be part of British Intelligence, Pat came to feel he was surrounded by "upper-class twits" who were avoiding active service. My father describes Pat's resignation thus: "When the kennel fees of two aristocratic cats were passed chargeable to the British government, Pat handed in his notice, went to Montreal, and walked into an RCAF recruiting office."

Pat's integrity was what made him feel he now had to fight in a personal capacity. Perhaps he could have contributed more with his brain, but no institution had yet found a way to harness that. Pat qualified as a navigator in the Royal Canadian Air Force. He could have avoided going to the front when the PMO tried again to enlist his services, but he insisted on completing his first tour of duty before he could accept their offer. He had to "do his bit" for decency and preserving a democratic way of life. On the night of December 24, 1944, over the Ruhr, the bomber in which he was the navigator, was caught in the flak. Pat urged his tail gunner to jump. He survived, but Pat went down with the plane and did not.

And so I was named in Pat's memory. My Godparents were Leonard Brockington and Jean Paterson (later Jean Crowe), Pat's widow. Jean was instrumental in finding me my first job, at the CBC. To honour her and my namesake, I have always been credited onscreen as W. Paterson Ferns.

The question I am most frequently asked is, "if you were born in Winnipeg, why did you grow up in England?" Here's why.

My father was a brilliant young scholar who chose Communism over Fascism while on his way to take up a scholarship at Cambridge University in England. He had attended the University of Manitoba, going on to Queen's University in Kingston for his Master's. In 1936 he was offered a job in the Civil Service, but discovered that he had won a scholarship from the International Order of the Daughters of the Empire which would enable him to attend Cambridge University.

He was advised to apply to Trinity College, a rich institution which had produced 80 percent of British Nobel laureates. He was accepted and so sailed for England on a Cunard steamship the *RMS Ausonia*, which is where this bright prairie innocent had his Damascus Road experience.

At dinner as the ship sailed up the St. Lawrence, Dad found himself in conversation with a retired Major from the Indian Army. They discussed events in Spain and the growth of Fascism in Europe. He gave my father *The Handbook of Marxism* to read, which produced a sudden surge of enlightenment. Dad had studied various revolutions including the English Civil War, the American Revolution, the French Revolution (but interestingly, not the Russian Revolution) and his conclusion was that each was a moral undertaking on the road to democracy and freedom. Marx, on the other hand, attached no moral imperative to such struggles, arguing that societies evolve without a dependence on moral order. Given what was happening in the world, what he was reading seemed to make sense and answer the questions then forming in his mind. Canada's development had been achieved by economic activity rather than by soldiers. Greed, more than morality, explained success.

With or without Marx, Dad was already on the road to an economic interpretation of history. The concept of the rule of markets did not reflect the real world, dominated as it was by vested interests and the wealthy. The notion of the triumph of the working class and a withering away of the state appealed to his young mind. Having seen the suffering of the Depression and the threats facing Europe, he did not find Marxism in conflict with the Judeo-Christian ideas with which he had grown up. A materialist vision of a world without God was easier to accept: In his own words, "a new and exhilarating arrogance was born."

"At that time," Dad continued, "the predominant tendency was to consider Marxism and the Communist International as one and indivisible—one doctrine and one church." He had become a convert. He would not leave this church until fifteen years later, when he encountered a learned Marxist scholar who was at the same time a very strong and lifelong anti-Communist.

Armed with his new faith in a world choosing between Communism and Fascism, he was ready to face the mysteries of Cambridge University. His Cambridge years, recounted in his autobiography *Reading from Left to Right*, are not my story, but his encounter with his Tutor G.S.R. Kitson Clark on his first day at Trinity resonates with me. Dad, who had been used to being treated kindly by his teachers, was not welcomed to the college by Kitson Clark, but rudely put down as a colonial and scolded for not wearing his gown. In my own career, I too was often dismissed as a colonial upstart by British broadcast executives, but I had my own defences, armed with my own first-class degree from Cambridge to dispel their initial assumptions. To be fair to Kitson Clark, it was he who encouraged my father to study Argentina for his PhD, which became a key academic focus in his life. My father graduated with a top first-class honours degree.

At Cambridge, my father was approached to join the student branch of the Communist Party, but told that he could not be an open member of the Party, could not have a party card, or participate in ordinary meetings, as overseas students were at greater risk, both in the United Kingdom and more importantly, given the consequences they might suffer, when they returned home. When Dad went home for the Long Vacation in 1938, he had a letter of introduction to Tim Buck, the leader of the Canadian Communist Party. His name was certainly in the files of the Communist Party. And when my mother went to visit Dad in Cambridge the following year, she recalls stuffing Communist literature in envelopes for circulation. She and Dad were secretly married during that visit, which I only discovered when we were celebrating their silver wedding anniversary and Jean Crowe let out the secret of their real wedding date. They were officially married in a church after my dad returned to Canada in 1940, and from that time on, he had no contact with anyone in the Party: he was a Marxist, but not a Communist.

When war broke out, my father had been examined by the Joint Recruiting Board and was deemed medically unfit on account of his deafness. He was recommended to a central agency as suitable for tasks of national importance given his experience and training. After spending some time continuing his studies at Harvard, Dad returned to Canada hoping to work for the Department of External Affairs in Ottawa, but his deafness was again cited as an impediment. He was referred to the Civil Service Commission which offered him a junior administrative post. He arrived in Ottawa in April 1940 as the "Phoney War" was coming to an end.

After ten days of filing index cards, Dad was asked to come to the Office of the Prime Minister, where he was to serve for three years, moving on to the External Affairs for a further eighteen months before he retired from public service. Obviously, he had top security clearance. He was the person who brought the message to Mackenzie King of the Japanese attack on Pearl Harbour. But his account of four years and seven months in the East Block was that it was a waste: "of my time, the taxpayers' money, office space, stenographic services, everything." He did not have a "good war" and felt the same applied to Brockington, Paterson, and many others. "Political intelligence in the Canadian government was characterized by boneheaded stupidity," he recalled.

After the war, in the summer of 1946, the Gouzenko spy scandal erupted. Igor Gouzenko, a defecting Communist, alleged the existence of a Soviet spy ring in Canada. My father's name was accused of appearing in Gouzenko's diaries, which referenced a "Paul Ferns," a scientist working in a laboratory in Montreal, and said that contact could be made through the British traitor Allan Nunn May (an old boy of my high school who had studied at

Cambridge). My father's first name was not Paul, he was not a scientist, never worked in a lab in Montreal, and never met Nunn May, who had left Cambridge before my Dad arrived. It would seem that the Soviet bureaucracy was no better than the Canadian one. When the Access to Information Act was passed in 1985, Dad had a colleague check the reference to him in Gouzenko's diaries and discovered that someone had mis-transcribed the Cyrillic: the person's name was not "Ferns" but "Ferris." So, as a result of a typographical error, my family moved to the UK and I received a British education. But I am jumping ahead.

After the war, my father returned to academic life to teach at United College in Winnipeg, then affiliated with the University of Manitoba. Exasperated by the journalism in the city's two newspapers, *The Winnipeg Free Press* and *The Winnipeg Tribune,* Dad conceived the idea that there should be a third newspaper. He rang his friend Dave Simkin, who with his father ran two firms: Universal Printers and the Israelite Press, which produced the *Israelite News.* The father had come to Canada from Russia before the First World War. He had been active in the Jewish Bund, a radical socialist movement fighting autocracy.

The challenge in starting any newspaper is capital. The young upstarts decided to take on the establishment by creating a cooperative newspaper to be called *The Winnipeg Citizen.* The paper commenced publication on March 1, 1948, and ceased publication on April 13, 1949. It is an exciting story, but not mine to tell. (Again, I refer you to my father's autobiography.)

What was to impact my life was that the existing newspapers did not relish the prospect of competition. While they preached support for free enterprise, free competition was for others, certainly not for the newspaper owners. When it was announced that my father was to be president of *The Winnipeg Citizen*, he was summoned by the Principal of United College, who was concerned that these activities might conflict with the financing efforts of the College, as the publisher of *The Winnipeg Tribune* chaired the College's fundraising committee. The upshot was that though my father subsequently resigned the Presidency of *The Winnipeg Citizen*, his job at United College was terminated. He managed to secure a contract for a more lucrative position at the University of Manitoba, which provoked a reaction among the newspaper proprietors, one of whom declared an intention "to run that son of a bitch Ferns out of town." After Dad appealed to the Board of Governors, the appointment was upheld, but only on a temporary basis.

While at the University of Manitoba, Dad was invited by Judge Stubbs, a famous Winnipeg radical, to address the Canadian-Soviet Friendship Society. My father rather pompously said he would speak as long as he was free to say what he thought and not be expected to engage in apologetics for the Soviet regime. His theme was one he had used before in addressing the United Nations Association while teaching at United College, namely that Canada was located between two superpowers and Canada's interest was to promote understanding between them. However, this was not a popular position: one had to be firmly anti-Soviet and 100 percent in favour of the United States.

Seeing that his future was far from secure at the University of Manitoba, Dad applied for a Social Science Research Grant to further his research on British enterprise in Argentina, which was to be the subject of his PhD thesis for Cambridge University and later his definitive economic history of Argentina, published as *Britain and Argentina in the Nineteenth Century* by Oxford University Press.

Needing access to a good library and armed with his grant, he was accepted by the Graduate School of the University of Chicago.

"The fascinating experience of living in Chicago and studying at the University of Chicago came suddenly to an end in the first week of August 1949," my father recalled. "My work was disrupted and my prospect of life in Canada was destroyed by the Canadian government."

In April 1949, my father had been offered a teaching post at the naval college at Royal Roads on Vancouver Island. My parents (who now had a third son) had sold their house in Winnipeg and made an offer on a house in Victoria, and my mother was preparing for our journey West. As a four-year-old, I remember being told that we would take a train, cross the Rocky Mountains, board a ferry, and go to live on an island. It was very exciting. Then Dad learned that his job was terminated before it had even begun.

Was it his politics? He was a Marxist, but no Communist. Or had Dad not been properly vetted and the government feared questions in Parliament about whether they had let a Soviet spy into the Royal Military College? Or was it the mistranscription in Gouzenko's diaries?

He went to see Mr. Justice A.K. Dysart, who spent twenty-six years as a judge of Manitoba's Court of Queen's Bench and five as a member of the Manitoba Court of Appeal. He read the correspondence between Dad, the Civil Service Commission, and the Royal Military College. When he was done, he said slowly and deliberately:

> Ferns, I am deeply ashamed of the advice I am going to give you. Many years on the Bench have persuaded me

> that one can never get justice from a government. They have too many resources at their command. Therefore, I advise you not to waste either your time or your money on a legal action for breach of contract. But I will do this. I shall write to Ottawa expressing my indignation at what they have done to you.

My father appealed to the Civil Service Commission who said this was a matter for the Department of Defence who in turn said it was a matter for the Civil Service Commission. In a meeting with the Department of Defence, Dad asked if it was anything to do with the speech he had given to the Canada-Soviet Friendship Society. The officer conceded that that might have had something to do with it. Whatever it was, the die was cast: He had to get out of the country. McCarthyism was rife south of the border and Canada, it seemed, was no different. Reds under the bed. In due course, my father received a meagre $2,000 in compensation. The cheque came not from the Civil Service Commission but from the Department of Defence.

Dad's prospects for a life in Canada were quashed. The family would now take a train east, board the Cunard liner *RMS Aquitania* and sail from Halifax to Southampton and, for the five of us, to a new life.

CHAPTER 2

CHILDHOOD, BOYHOOD, YOUTH (1949–1968)

FROM SOUTHAMPTON IN THE south of England, we travelled north to Scotland to Muckle Shore on the North Sea coast east of Aberdeen. One of my few memories is sitting on the top of a double-decker bus in Aberdeen and being told that the Queen Mother was driving past. I pretended I had seen her. Soon we were heading south to take up residence in "Little Tunbridge," a rented bungalow in the village of Botisham off the Newmarket Road, six miles from Cambridge. The place names surrounding us were exotic: Caxton Gibbet, Lode, Six Mile Bottom, Stow cum Qy, and Swaftham Bulbeck. I was sent to the Kindergarten across the street at the Village College. This was indeed a whole new world, especially daunting for my elder brother John, who had already started school in Canada, and of no import to my younger brother Chris, still a baby.

Post-war Britain was a land of deprivation and ration books, a difficult situation for my parents, who had had to sell off most of the furniture which they had accumulated in Winnipeg.

One possession that did accompany us was a green Chrysler pedal-car which had been my only present the previous Christmas. But it was in Botisham that I learned to ride a bicycle, which proved much more useful when fourteen years later I was myself to study at Cambridge University.

After Dad's year of research in Cambridge, he secured a job in 1950 as a lecturer at Birmingham University, where he spent the balance of his career, rising to become Dean of the Faculty of Commerce and Social Science. Given our family's minimal resources, we travelled to Birmingham in the back of the moving van along with what little furniture we had. I recall Chris throwing a shoe from his only pair of shoes out of the van while en route.

Our home for the next dozen years was 49 Paradise Lane in Hall Green, a suburb on the south side of Birmingham, where a housing development had grown up alongside an old farm house and a block of labourers' cottages. It seemed pretty idyllic: trails along the lane, and nearby the Sarehole Mill and "The Dingles," where Tolkien imagined the characters for *The Hobbit* and *Lord of the Rings*.

What was less idyllic was the air we had to breathe. Situated in the heart of the "Black Country," Britain's "Second City" was incredibly polluted. There were pea-souper fogs and smogs, in which my parents literally had to feel their way home. When Mum hung out the sheets to dry, they would come back speckled black with soot. Coming from the clean cold air of the Prairies, my metabolism could not handle the pollution. I contracted bronchitis and was in bed for eight weeks. The next winter it was seven weeks, the next six, and so on. After eight years I grew accustomed to the pollution, though to be fair, the government had passed a Clean Air Act in 1956.

Despite the air pollution, Birmingham had much to offer, especially on the cultural front. My Mum took me to concerts at the Town Hall to hear the City of Birmingham Symphony Orchestra. The Town Hall was an ugly black building, but when it was restored and air pollution was under control, it re-emerged as a beautiful white replica of the Parthenon. The Birmingham Repertory Theatre had a superb reputation. I saw the young Albert Finney in *Macbeth* (and was spattered with blood in the front row) and Ian Richardson's *Hamlet.* The Royal Shakespeare Company's Memorial Theatre was just twenty miles away in Stratford-upon-Avon where I saw Charles Laughton's *King Lear*, and, years later, Paul Scofield's; talents such as Vanessa Redgrave and Judi Dench, Laurence Olivier and the other knights of the stage. I saw my first opera at the Theatre Royal on New Street. When we wanted to attend such events that were beyond the modest pocket money we received, we would ask Dad for a "cultural subsidy." Most often it was granted.

Living on the south side of the city we were inclined to support Birmingham City Football Club rather than Aston Villa. Soccer (or football as it is called in England) excites religious commitment. I have kept faith with the Blues even to this day, but it was my introduction to pain and suffering which continues unabated. Having been relegated from the elite Premier League, and from the Championship to soccer's third tier, the team still languishes… though an infusion of American cash may redeem it.

My education began in the state system with fifty children in a class, with a couple of years in infant school followed by four years in Junior School and then the notorious 11+ exam. At Hall Green Junior School, I was the top boy, but not until my final year did I beat the top girl. It was known that girls develop faster than boys. What was less well known was that one's educational fate was often decided at the tender age of seven. In my school, the "A" stream passed the 11+ exam and would go to grammar school; the "C" stream did not and would go to a secondary modern school (later called comprehensive schools). These streams were put in place at the end of infant school. Very few children changed streams in the four years of Junior School. Thus, you were put on an academic track or destined for trade school before you were even taught multiplication tables. Hall Green was a middle-class area. I am sure that in the slums of Birmingham, the percentages hoping for an academic future were slender.

After sitting the 11+ in 1956, I took the examination to attend King Edward's School, Birmingham, then just over 400 years old. It was what was called a "direct grant" school. These were independent selective schools which charged fees, but received government grants in return for admitting poorer pupils (like me) who were nominated by the local authorities and whose fees were paid by the government. Each year, KES took the top seventy-five students from a city of two million. When the system financing education was changed by a Labour government in the mid-1970s, direct grant schools were abolished. Most became independent schools that subsisted on the fees they charged.

The KES teaching staff in my era were all graduates of Oxford and Cambridge, and KES was consistently at or near the top of *The Times* listings of the best schools in the country. It was truly a privileged education. Unlike most public schools (which are the exclusive private schools such as Eton and Harrow) there were no boarders, but we competed with the public schools in academics, in sports and other activities.

There was a richness of extracurricular activities and sports galore: rugby in the winter and cricket in the summer, plus all manner of individual sports from tennis and swimming to Eton fives. There was a shooting range. All on a campus with science labs, music rooms, gymnasia, etc. Across the main school drive, these facilities were duplicated for an equivalent girls' school. But in those days, the divide was rarely crossed.

We attended school on five weekdays and on Saturday morning. Most Tuesday and Thursday afternoons were devoted to sport, and Friday afternoon to the Combined Cadet Force (Army, Navy, and Air Force). The school was divided into eight houses which competed in sports on the weekday afternoons. School teams competed with other schools on Saturday afternoons. And there was homework, a lot of it.

KES was on the other side of Birmingham from where we lived, so I took three different buses each morning to get to school and three to get home. It was only in the sixth form, my final year, that Dad acquired a car, so I could occasionally get a ride to school. We did not have a TV until I was leaving school for my "gap year." Hence, I was a voracious reader.

Coming from a family of high academic achievers, I saw my education as a seemingly endless series of hurdles. Be top of the class, get in to KES, get good "O" levels, get good "A" levels, get into Oxford or Cambridge, get a good degree … when would it ever end? But while I worked hard, I also benefitted from everything King Edward's had to offer. I played for the school cricket teams at all levels and rugby in the earlier grades; I played for the house teams. I was house captain and a school prefect; I conducted the house orchestra and choir; I performed in junior school plays and senior school plays. I sang in the school choir, and I was the drum major in the combined cadet force band.

Let me share a couple of experiences that propelled me towards the arts. In my first year at KES (1956–1957) the junior school play was *Androcles and the Lion* by George Bernard Shaw. I had four small parts (a slave, a peasant, a shepherd, and the like) for which my mother made the costumes. (For the senior school plays, we rented the costumes from the Shakespeare Memorial Theatre in near-by Stratford-upon-Avon.) Three weeks before the production, the boy playing Androcles broke his leg. In a surprise move, the master directing the play asked me to step into the lead. I learned all my lines with my Mum in the rock garden of Paradise Lane, but I also had to learn to dance (with the lion). A young master brought in his fiancée to assist with the choreography, a daunting prospect for a twelve-year-old. He would scatter desks and chairs throughout the geography room and tell me to lead my dance partner through this obstacle course, "encouraging" me with instructions. ("Hold her closer. I'm not jealous.") I inherited my costume from the boy with the broken leg. He was two years older than me and much bigger, so despite my mother's efforts to adapt it, it looked pretty ill-fitting and her four costumes were worn with panache by others. Still, the production was a success.

Our senior school plays were of such calibre that they were occasionally reviewed by theatre critics from London. One compared our production of Ben Jonson's *Volpone* with Sir Donald Wolfit's production in the West End, which provoked the master directing the play to write to *The Daily Telegraph* (I believe it was) to remind the critic that these were schoolboys, not professional actors. Those school plays taught me standards of excellence that served me well throughout my career.

In my final year (1962–1963), the age of satire was raging, and I thought we should stage a revue. There had been two previous revues, one directed by Nathan Joseph, who went on to the Presidency of TransAtlantic Records, and the second by Bill Oddie, a contemporary of my elder brother, who became one of *The Goodies*, a BBC comedy show. The revue I organized was titled *The End of the Line*. I co-wrote it with my sixth form colleagues, had a starring role and promoted the hell out of it. There were two sold-out performances. The Chief Master hid himself in the organ loft to watch our opening night, and once he saw that the satire was rarely directed at him, he came publicly to the second performance full of pride for this "daring" undertaking.

One other experience worth recording was my desire to be chosen to read one of the lessons in the school's Christmas service of nine lessons and carols. Each year I auditioned and was given the Adam and Eve story to read. When I got to the line "Adam took the apple and ate," I would always pronounce the last word "eight," in my Canadian accent, and I didn't get the part. In my final year, determined to be selected, I abandoned my colonial reading and pronounced "eight" as "et" in an impeccable English accent. I got the part. On the night, I did not revert to my colonial roots, but played the good assimilated Englishman and delivered my "et" in the proper and accepted manner.

My final year was devoted to securing a place at Oxford or Cambridge. It was still the era before combined university entrance applications, so I applied separately to various groups of Cambridge colleges including my father's alma mater Trinity College, and some Oxford Colleges including St. Edmund Hall, from which my brother John had graduated. John had not been accepted at Trinity and neither was I, in my case because my Latin was not up to snuff. (Later, my younger brother Chris did get accepted by Trinity, but that is another story.) After the written examinations and interviews I was accepted by Pembroke College, Cambridge, and by "Teddy Hall," Oxford, John's alma mater.

I intended to take a "gap year" before starting college and deciding whether to study English, as I had hoped, or Economics, as Dad was urging me. Oxford wanted me to make my decision right away, so I chose Cambridge, which was willing to wait.

For my gap year (1963–1964) I wanted to go to Canada to discover my native land, and I managed to secure a position as a student teacher at Glenlyon Preparatory School in Victoria, British Columbia. Founded in 1932 by a Scotsman, Major Ian Simpson, the school campus was on a beautiful oceanside property on Beach Drive in Oak Bay and the main building was once the home of the notorious architect Francis Rattenbury, who designed the British Columbia Legislature and Victoria's Empress Hotel. His celebrity came from the fine buildings he created; his notoriety came from a scandalous divorce and being murdered in England at the age of sixty-seven by his second wife's lover.

The school offered board and lodging and a modest salary. It was the first time I had any money to spend. I resided in the Rattenbury Coach House along with two other teachers. The major's impressive wife Florence ruled the roost. The major's son Hamish, who was sharing the role of headmaster that year prior to taking over for his father, became a lifelong friend. He grew the school, which in my time went from grade 3 to 10, and turned it from a family business into an independent foundation. Years later Glenlyon amalgamated with an equivalent girls' school, Norfolk House, to form a co-educational School. Hamish went on to be the principal of the Lester B. Pearson College of the Pacific, and subsequently headmaster at the Prep School at Upper Canada College in Toronto.

A subsequent graduate of Glenlyon was filmmaker Atom Egoyan. Hamish Simpson told him to contact me when he reached Toronto. Atom came to my office with a rucksack full of his home movies. I was entranced and wrote a letter of recommendation to the Canada Council to secure his first grant. When I wrote congratulating him on winning the Jury Prize in Cannes for *Exotica*, he generously wrote back saying, "You were the first."

At Glenlyon, I was to teach grades 3 and 4, as well as grade 10 French and social studies. Grade 10 was a challenge as the boys were only three years younger than me and many were taller (and, I presumed, stronger). My approach to teaching was to educate and entertain, hoping to achieve the former through a judicious use of the latter. "Make them laugh and they will learn." Of course, in the contemporary educational system, no untrained teacher would be allowed near a classroom, but I had a great time. The boys and their parents were good to me and for the first time in years, I did not have much homework, just keeping ahead of the grade 10 students in social studies. But I had a lot of homework to mark. I also took games: rugby, soccer, and cricket.

Enjoying a freedom that was long overdue, I bought a twelve-string guitar and a five-string banjo and taught myself to play. It was the beginning of the folk music craze, so I purchased records of Pete Seeger, Bob Dylan, Peter, Paul and Mary, and my favourites, Canada's own Ian and Sylvia. Ian Tyson had attended Glenlyon School, and I was later to work with Sylvia Tyson staging the first folk/country concert at Roy Thomson Hall in Toronto. In Victoria, I became a folk singer, performing at the Secret Coffee House in the basement of the Douglas Hotel.

During that year at Glenlyon, I fell in love with my country of origin and vowed that after Cambridge I would return. I had tasted the freedom of living away from home. I had made friends among the staff and students. And I had maintained a regular correspondence with my first and only girlfriend back in the UK.

Jenny eventually became my wife and the mother of our three children. She had a longing to escape home, and indeed England, so it was not difficult to persuade her to share my view of Canada as a promised land.

My love for Canada increased during a cross-country trip I took on the way back to the UK.

With one of my teacher friends, we drove through the Rockies to Calgary for the Stampede, where we were joined by Hamish Simpson. We all slept in the basement of my Uncle Don's home. Thereafter, Don and his family drove me across the prairies to Winnipeg. There I stayed with my paternal grandparents, who in turn drove me through endless forests to Toronto, where I met my Godfather Leonard Brockington for the only time. He had an office in the Lord Simcoe Hotel. Its walls were lined with photos of himself with world leaders of various descriptions. My eye was drawn to a file card referencing him, which a soldier liberating Hitler's bunker had pulled from the Führer's files. Brockington had been one of Canada's most prominent orators and propagandists during the War, giving Churchillian speeches on radio in his mellifluous Welsh tones.

From Toronto I took a bus to New York, where I visited the 1964 World's Fair at Flushing Meadows. I sailed back to England on a Holland America ocean liner, arriving in Southampton just in time for my elder brother's wedding. He and his bride were heading to Canada, where he would do his Master's degree at Western in London, Ontario. Like me, John and my younger brother would return to Canada, with John making his career principally at McMaster University in Hamilton, and Chris at Mount St. Vincent in Halifax. My sister Eleanor, eleven years younger than me, remained in England, her country of birth, as did my parents. Eleanor married a lawyer who had studied at Cambridge.

I went up to Pembroke College in the fall of 1964 and decided to accede to my father's wishes to read economics. At the end of my first term I was totally confused and admitted to my father that I was lost. His advice was to read the classics: Marx, Marshall, Schumpeter, Keynes, and the like. This did not help. But I applied myself, and did well enough in Part One of the Economics Tripos that my tutor told me I had just missed getting first class honours. I excitedly reported this to my father, whose response was "What went wrong?" Wrong? I am at heart a very competitive person and from that point I was determined to show him that nothing "went wrong." At the end of my three years at Cambridge, in Part Two, I took a top first-class honours degree and won the Wrenbury Scholarship, which would support me wherever I chose to take my Master's. Put that in your pipe and smoke it, Dad!

I played soccer for the college, attended debates at the Union, but my most important extra-curricular activity was Footlights. Founded in 1882, this student drama group specialized in staging revues. Thanks to the 1960s satire boom and recent successes at the Edinburgh Festival, it was a club in hot demand. Half of the cast of *Beyond the Fringe*, Peter Cook and Jonathan Miller, were from Footlights, and its members would go on to dominate British comedy, creating such series as *Monty Python's Flying Circus*, *The Goodies*, *Not Only... But Also*, *I'm Sorry, I'll Read That Again*, *At Last the 1948 Show*, *That Was the Week That Was*, and *The Hitchhiker's Guide to the Galaxy*. The 1981 revue alone would feature Emma Thompson, Hugh Laurie, and Stephen Fry.

In my first year, I appeared in the Pembroke "Smoker" (so named because one wore black tie, or a "smoking jacket"), a college revue trying out material for the annual Footlights revue at the Arts Theatre. The revue generally travelled to the Edinburgh

Fringe Festival, and success could lead to a West End engagement in London. Our cast was Footlights' president Eric Idle of *Monty Python* fame, future TV critic and host Clive James, Germaine Greer (she being the first female member of Footlights), me, and one other person whom I cannot recall, with music by John Cameron, who went on to orchestrate the hit musical *Les Miserables*. In the large room under the Pembroke College Library, there was a sizeable audience and red wine was flowing, a combination that led to explosive laughter.

A highlight was Germaine's striptease. Dressed as a nun, she swung her rosary as she peeled off her habit and reduced the crowd to tears. Initially reluctant to return the following year as she was studying for her final exams, she agreed to do one number immediately before the interval ... but she would not rehearse. She arrived carrying a huge hatbox in which was a large piece of decorative headgear featuring a life-sized stuffed pigeon. She handed sheet music to John Cameron. She sang *Rule Britannia*, but through some strange contortion, her lips and the words she sang were out of sync. It was truly extraordinary and brought the house down. An encore was demanded. Germaine obliged by repeating the performance, but this time with hand gestures that were out of sync with both her lips and the music. It was a once-in-a-lifetime experience.

During my time at Cambridge, I formed a folk/cabaret group with Martin Baily, a close friend from KES. We added a girl singer, the very talented Diana Lubbock, and our name was (imaginatively) Two 'n' One. In one of our early rehearsals we were talking about our birthdays, Martin and me both having been born on January 13, 1945. In an extraordinary coincidence, Diana revealed that she too was born on that day in the same year. We thought that the stars had aligned and that fate had destined us for greatness. Though we made a demo disc with songs composed by Martin and me, and hawked it around record companies in London, we did not "make it." However, in our final year we added Jim King as a bongo player, and were invited to perform at various May Balls. We were the ninth and final group on the billing for the May Ball at Martin's college, Christ's, behind an amazing line-up of talent. Top of the bill was The Who. They were preparing to go to the Monterey Pop Festival, now immortalized on film. This was the time when they smashed up their instruments at the end of their performance. I vividly recall hearing them from the front row and watching Pete Townshend leaving the stage with blood dripping from his hands. In later life, I could boast to my kids that I had played on the same bill as The Who. And then, later in my career, I had the pleasure of actually working with the amazing lead singer Roger Daltrey.

Martin and Jim, like me, read economics and we all earned first class degrees. The different careers we pursued were a testament to the breadth of approaches one could take in the Economics Tripos. Martin used sophisticated mathematical formulae in his work teaching at MIT and Yale, was recruited by McKinsey, and served as chair of the economic council in Bill Clinton's cabinet. Jim used statistics, and formed his own statistical research company. I avoided formulae and numbers as much as I could by focusing on political sociology, economic history, and the like. When I went into business, what I took from Cambridge was a capacity for hard work and an ability to write. So much of education these days seems to depend on checking off fixed choice answers, whereas I had to write two or more often three essays a week throughout my time at Cambridge.

I also attribute my academic success to an ability to flourish under the stress of examinations. Each Cambridge final exam, whether in macro-economics, micro-economics, or the comparative economic history of India and Japan, required four essays written in the space of three hours. I became expert at predicting on the basis of past exam papers what the subjects might be: whether some area had been neglected and was due to come up, what was currently hot, what were the enthusiasms of the examiner. Different dons set the exams, and one had a fair idea (but no certainty) who the examiner would be. I had prepared index cards with multiple essay plans for each subject: the sum total of my knowledge was contained in a pack of cards. In my first exam I had plans for essays on two of the questions asked and something that could be adapted for a third. Thus, I only had to "think" for one essay. For the next exam I had three fully correct predictions out of four. Thereafter it was all four.

At Cambridge, it is a requirement in university exams that the examiner be present at the start of the exam to release the examination papers. In one instance I had predicted that a right-wing economist was setting the paper. Instead, professor Joan Robinson, a Keynesian, walked into the room. So, metaphorically I switched from a Tory "blue" pen to a socialist "red" pen and was able to adapt what I wrote to be more in sympathy with her ideological beliefs. I was learning how to sell my "ideas."

It was a relief to get the first-class honours degree I sought and a scholarship to boot for my future studies. I chose to study in 1967–1968 at the newly created Centre for Contemporary Cultural Studies, which Richard Hoggart had just established at Birmingham University. I did not want to be sucked into academic life, and this was one of the few institutions where one could get a master's degree in a single year. Hoggart's claim to fame was his publication of *The Uses of Literacy* in 1957. Partly autobiography, the volume was interpreted as lamenting the loss of an authentic working-class popular culture in Britain, and denouncing the imposition of a mass culture through advertising, media, and Americanization. He was also the star witness in the 1960 trial of *Lady Chatterley's Lover* that ended British censorship of that novel. I wrote my thesis on *Sociology and Film* which, I have always claimed, "cured me" of sociology for life. I included a first chapter written in the impenetrable language of sociology, just to show that I had studied the concepts. After that it was relatively sensible. And it did give me a chance to watch films for a year. I was able to live cheaply at home, and Jenny was studying at Keele University, near Stoke-on-Trent, north of Birmingham, so I could visit her each weekend. Hers was a four-year course that included a Certificate in Education, an essential teaching qualification. By then we had become engaged to be married and had definitely decided to move to Canada.

The additional challenge of my Master's year was to find a job in Canada. I was interested in the National Film Board of Canada, recommended by my godfather Leonard Brockington and by Graham Spry (the godfather of the CBC), then working for the Saskatchewan Government in London. With these impeccable sponsors and encouraging correspondence from the film commissioner, I felt confident I would be offered something. But nothing happened, while in the meantime, Jenny had secured a teaching position in Montreal.

In desperation, I wrote my godmother Jean Crowe to ask her to send me the address of the Canadian Broadcasting Corporation in Toronto. She replied that she only knew one person at the CBC and his name was Richard Nielsen. I wrote to him. His response was a twenty-minute phone call, at the end of which he hired me as his Director of Research for a new weekend series he was confident of getting. He liked my handwriting and remembered letters my father had written to the *Globe and Mail.* Hardly solid grounds for employment. As it turned out, Dick was not given the weekend series, but was asked to continue running *The Public Eye*, a half-hour weekly current affairs series, along with a monthly documentary slot imaginatively called *Document.* The only conditions Dick imposed were that I report for work in six weeks' time.

My problem was I still had to take my university exams, which I managed to bring forward. I had to complete my thesis. And I had to get married. I negotiated that if I came to Toronto for eight weeks, I could take a two-week break in order to fly back to Birmingham, get married, and rush to board a Canadian Pacific steamship from Liverpool to Montreal, with a honeymoon in bunk beds! That became the pace of my future life in Canada. I naively thought that once my education was complete, my evenings would be free, but it was not to be.

One's formative years set patterns for the rest of life. When we arrived in England, we were perceived as Americans, who were not well liked. Attitudes changed when we explained we were from Canada, but that did not mean we were accepted. We were colonials. Of course, so much in the UK is about class, and how one speaks usually denotes where you come from and to which class you belong. We were outsiders, and ever since then I feel I have always been an outsider. When I returned to Canada, people assumed I was English because of my accent, which I suppose is now a mid-Atlantic mixture. Thus, I am a colonial in the mother country and perceived as a foreigner in Canada. I did not "belong." And I never have. A professional orphan, I guess. But my sense of independence was born.

CHAPTER 3

MOTHER CORP (1968–1972)

I ARRIVED IN CANADA ON the day of the first federal party leaders' debate on national television, co-produced by the CBC/Radio-Canada and CTV. The leaders of Canada's four main political parties faced off in this debate: Progressive Conservative leader Robert Stanfield, New Democratic Party leader Tommy Douglas, Réal Caouette, leader of the Social Credit Party, and the new Prime Minister, Liberal leader Pierre Elliott Trudeau, at the height of "Trudeaumania."

The next morning, I reported for duty at 135 Maitland Street in Toronto on June 10, 1968. The building, in white tile, reminded me of a public urinal. Down the street was the elegant old Quaker Meeting House, then serving as the National Ballet School. I took the elevator to the fourth floor which housed the units of *The Public Eye* and *Newsmagazine*. *Take 30* was on the third floor, and, as I later discovered, the CBC top brass were either on the sixth floor or down Jarvis Street in a place known as "The Kremlin." As the elevator opened, I was met by a hostile presence in the form of Dick Nielsen's assistant Anne Emin. She was an Armenian of immense talent, but public relations were not among her skills. She was fiercely defensive of Dick and doubtless thought my appointment was another of his "enthusiasms" (for which read "acts of madness"). Anne guarded Dick's office as if it was the Oval Office, in complete contrast to Dick's easy-going openness. However, she proved to be a huge ally, surreptitiously helping the two of us when we were plotting our escape from the CBC four years later. Anne went on to greater things at Mother Corporation, and they would be blessed in having her qualities of administration, organization, and leadership.

Anne introduced me to my new assistant (yes, the Director of Research had an assistant!), a gorgeous sari-clad Indian, Maqbool Jung. Anne clearly saw Maqbool as another of Dick's acts of madness, and though bright and quick-witted, Maqbool's languid, laid-back style proved hardly the right fit for a hard-hitting investigative current affairs program. She eventually married Michael Spencer, the executive director of Telefilm Canada, and proved to be a wonderful lifelong companion.

I am sure Anne's initial impression of me was influenced by my grey suit, white shirt, and tie in the midst of a hot and humid Toronto summer. I quickly adapted to the more casual dress code of the unit. Dick took me for lunch my first day with a few others, and I quickly realized that such gatherings were where ideas were launched, explored, and accepted or rejected. It was a place where the guests had access to Dick and where I, for one, could benefit from Dick's formidable experience and intelligence. I proved a good listener and Dick became my mentor.

We later discovered that Dick was a "talker" rather than a "speaker." If there were more than half a dozen people to address, he became uncomfortable and I was usually called upon to do the presentation. Dick seemed to lead by talking: on the telephone, over lunch, or in his office with his feet up on his desk. I quickly realized that I had a lot to learn. I had grown up in the Mother Country and had to get up to speed on Canadian politics, Canadian history, and how to be productive in my ill-defined new job. But I was ready for anything and everything.

When Dick asked me to research various ideas he wanted to pursue, I found that I had to move beyond my Cambridge training, which had encouraged book learning and written correspondence. In my new role, I needed to use the telephone and rely on contacts to generate the kind of research that would be suitable for a current affairs program where the emphasis was on "current." Maqbool did not welcome typing for me, and I had never learned to type, so very quickly I adapted to using the phone. But it did take an effort … Cultural change, I discovered, is hard!

I had eight weeks to make a mark before I flew home to get married. And I still had to arrange the typing of my Master's thesis while in Toronto. Meanwhile, one of the subjects Dick had asked me to research was the concept of "Mid-Canada" as articulated by Richard Rohmer: not the "civilised" Canada huddled within a hundred miles of the US border, nor the "North" of ice and tundra. Mid-Canada was the belt of the country that included the Canadian Shield and all the resource-rich towns on which the wealth of the nation seemed to depend. I started to read *The Northern Miner* and similar publications. And given that we made television shows, Dick thought I should go out on location to see how things were done.

I was assigned to producer Don Cumming who was to shoot some interviews in Northern Ontario for what would become the Mid-Canada show. And that's how I got my first break.

We were filming in Red Lake, Ontario, on the day that the Ontario brewery workers ended their strike. Everyone in town saw this as an opportunity to buy beer and celebrate. We were shooting in the main street when a gang of drunken youths approached the crew and started to become objectionable. Don Cumming would never shirk from a confrontation, so he took them on to his own cost and ended up in hospital. That left me with the duties of the producer, who in those days was in effect the director, writer, and interviewer. Somehow, I pulled it off. I leaned heavily on the cameraman to make directorial decisions, and pretended to know what I was doing. I feel as if I have been faking it ever since.

My biggest worry during that shoot were black flies, then in season and at their height. I was able to fend them off, but took a ring of bites around my neck. I had a vision of being at the altar getting married with everyone looking at my raw red neck. So, with great willpower, I resisted the urge to scratch and was able to walk down the aisle confident that my bride and not my neck would be the major attraction.

My two weeks' "vacation" was a whirlwind. Marriage, delivering my thesis, packing, saying goodbye to friends. We sailed on the *Empress of Canada* from Liverpool to Montreal with a brief stop in Quebec city. We were met in Montreal by my uncle Colin, the chief actuary for Prudential, then boarded a train for Toronto with a mountain of baggage. I had foolishly relied on Maqbool to make a reservation at a boarding house I had selected in Toronto. We arrived at Union Station to be given a message that somehow Maqbool had been unable to complete this task or to let me know. Instead my godmother persuaded a young friend to let us sleep on the floor of his apartment on the top floor of an apartment building with no elevator. In the unfamiliar and intense humidity, we struggled up four flights of stairs with trunks and suitcases. Next morning, we found a boarding house in the annex and moved our belongings. The following day Jenny found a job teaching grades 12 and 13 science at Vaughan Road Collegiate. The day after that we rented an apartment near the school. And this was to be the pace of our lives ever since!

In those two weeks away, much had happened at *The Public Eye*. Dick had fired our host Warner Troyer and was urgently looking for a replacement. As it turned out, he found five replacements, a rotating group of hosts including Peter Jennings, who went on to become the anchor at ABC News and Jeanne Sauvé, who later became governor general. Meanwhile, producer Robert Patchell had been doing a film on Czechoslovakia and was caught up in the Soviet occupation. It was 1968 and all hell was breaking loose. What a time to be thrown in the deep end of current affairs and investigative journalism.

Dick was also handed a monthly one-hour documentary series, called with the CBC's usual panache, *Document*. He had invited film director Peter Pearson, fresh from the success of his *The Best Damn Fiddler from Calibogie to Kaladar*, to take a leave of absence from the National Film Board to make one of these specials. I was assigned to Peter as his assistant, and it turned out to be quite an education.

Peter's girlfriend at the time was Margot Kidder, later Lois Lane of *Superman* fame. (The one time in my life I may have taken drugs—unknowingly—was when Margot offered me one of her chocolate brownies.) Peter did not work at the CBC offices, but fashionably had a studio which he shared with visual artist Jurgen Lutz in a downtown warehouse. Peter was definitely a part of the contemporary "Toronto scene," such a contrast with what seemed to me a repressed city, "Toronto the Good," where one had to fill in a form to buy booze, and restaurants' liquor licences were restricted on Sundays. The film Peter wanted to make was an exploration of youth dissent and protest in this turbulent era of sex, drugs, and rock 'n' roll, plus Vietnam protests and student revolution.

Peter's protagonist and "narrative glue" for the film was Margaret, a young Catholic girl from Quebec city who had dropped out of the University of Ottawa and was now living with an underground filmmaker in New York. We would have Margaret talk about her life and decisions and film her meeting a diverse group of "experts" commenting on the current turbulence, from anthropologist Margaret Mead to militant feminist Ti-Grace Atkinson. Our protagonist would reflect on her parents, her priests, her teachers, and why she dropped out. There would be a parade of politicians, sociologists, and the like to add to the commentary. As one of this dissenting generation, Margaret would stand on Parliament Hill to test what words were acceptable on mainstream television … from "bloody hell" to the F-word. What was actually permissible in a permissive age?

It was a complex of concepts and provocative ideas that Peter had generated and it was clear from the shooting that we had all the makings of a very good film, but perhaps only 90 percent of what was needed for a *great* film. Peter wanted to edit the film himself, which was not one of his better ideas, but had the effect of drawing me more closely into the filmmaking process in my new role as assistant editor. We would discuss differing structures: the format was flexible, but something was missing. I would assemble our changes overnight for us to screen a new version next morning. Feeling film in my hands, and the satisfaction of splicing 16mm film together, helped me to better understand the medium and learn the value of the length of a shot. Peter and I kept making and remaking the film until it was almost physically impossible to run the comprehensively taped workprint through the Movieola. But eventually it was finished … or at least we abandoned further efforts at restructuring.

The film's title was *If I Don't Agree, Must I Go Away?* for which Peter had Margaret write the title question on a steamed-up bathroom mirror after a shower. This cured me of ever using long, obscure titles or shooting extended title sequences during filming. We all called the film *Margaret.*

One sequence that was to prove controversial was of Margaret's boyfriend, the underground filmmaker, shooting a young couple in a bathtub. Clearly, they would not be wearing clothes in such a soft-core porno film, but our version for the CBC was discreet, implying nudity but never exposing any "naughty bits." It was a semi-satirical sequence of the "great man" at work, to which we added epic music from *Gone with the Wind.*

At the first screening for the CBC brass, Dick's supervisor Hugh Gauntlet raised his eyebrows and expressed concern about the "nude" scene. He had it screened for his superior John Kerr, a staunch Catholic. John did not like the film, nor the scene in question. So it went up to John's boss, department head Knowlton Nash. Knowlton's creative contribution to the discussion was that there were too many faucet shots. Would he have preferred nipples instead?

Next up the chain of command was Peter Campbell, erudite, witty, and gay. He read the tea leaves of this bureaucratic succession of avoiding responsibility, but nonetheless passed the buck to his own superior Marce Munro. Surprisingly, Marce was less troubled by the scene. He had been told that the naked couple had been facing each other in the tub, whereas what he saw was a male sitting behind the female whose back was towards him. This observation prompted Peter Campbell to utter the immortal lines: "I don't want to be outrageously inventive, Marce, but considerable damage could be done in that position!"

Perhaps inevitably, the "problem" was referred to Eugene Hallman, the head of the CBC English Network. Peter and I were asked to report to a screening room on Front Street where we showed the film to our fearless leader. At the conclusion of the screening, Hallman shook Peter's hand and mine and said what a fine film it was. By the time Peter and I had returned to the *Document* office, we learned that Hallman had banned the film.

What the CBC brass had failed to appreciate was that this was a co-production with the New York PBS station WNET. On learning this, there were comments that Dick Nielsen had behaved "like an Armenian carpet salesman" and in doing so had compromised the CBC. But films cost money, one needs partners, and contracts are contracts. WNET loved the film and would run it despite the CBC's hesitations. The US broadcast elicited a rave review from *The New York Times*. So, the various layers of the CBC bureaucracy had to reconsider the situation. Reluctantly they conceded that the film could be broadcast, faucet shots and all! The Canadian media response was "what was all the fuss about?"

For me, it was a quick course in understanding large bureaucratic organizations, and the CBC in particular. While my youthful ambition may have been to end up as president of the CBC, I now realized that my independence could not thrive in such an environment, where it was all about control and not creativity.

The first seeds were planted, both for Dick and for me, that we might have to escape. It turned out we were both outsiders.

Before the year was over, I had produced my first show for *The Public Eye* and Dick was finally asked to lead the new weekend public affairs initiative *CBC Weekend* which he thought he was getting a year earlier when he first hired me. There was a history of prominent public affairs shows that occupied the Sunday night time slot. The most famous of these was *This Hour Has Seven Days*, created by Doug Leiterman and Patrick Watson. It was launched in October 1964 and ran until it was controversially cancelled in April 1966. Capitalizing on the satire boom, it combined sketches and songs with hard news, politics, documentary, and discussion. Watson took over as co-host when John Drainie took ill, joining co-hosts Laurier Lapierre and Dinah Christie. *This Hour Has Seven Days* played a major role in bringing to public attention issues that had been suppressed or made taboo both in television and society as a whole.

The demise of *Seven Days* led to the creation of *Document*, the one-hour series of documentaries curated by Watson and Leiterman (which Dick inherited in 1968) and a magazine show called *Sunday*, under Daryl Duke. This was co-hosted by Robert Hoyt, Larry Zolf, and Peter Reilly and featured songs by Leonard Cohen and Ian Tyson. It lasted one season, to be succeeded by *The Way It Is*, executive produced by Ross Maclean. Hosted by academic John Saywell and former script assistant Jan Tennant, it was given a second season, the reason I started my career with a year on *The Public Eye* and *Document*.

The strength of CBC programming was its continuing series, the flagship weekend current affairs magazines, and the weekly *Newsmagazine*; *The Nature of Things*, its science series; *Man Alive*, its religious slot; *Take Thirty* in the afternoon: and subsequently, *The Fifth Estate*, its investigative unit was established. Factual programming was Canadian and found audience. Sports were strong, but drama and entertainment weak. Audiences looked to the USA for their fiction and situation comedy. What CBC lacked was a diversity of creativity, which an independent sector could have provided.

So Dick finally had the weekend public affairs show he thought he was getting when he hired me—under the title *CBC Weekend*. It turned out to be a poisoned chalice. The CBC decided there would be shows on both Saturday and Sunday: the former, lighter in tone, headed by Neil Andrews and employing a lot of very young contributors, and the latter, more substantial, headed by Dick with his crew of more seasoned producers who had been with him on *The Public Eye*. The hosts were Lloyd Robertson and Kay Sigurjonsson—a good mix. As there was a news element to both shows, a third executive was appointed to supervise that. I was not privy to their deliberations but I knew the troika structure was dysfunctional and Dick hated it. On top of all this was the oppressive bureaucracy I had witnessed with Peter's documentary. But I was now a producer on *CBC Weekend*, and this new role offered opportunity.

For three years I contributed stories to *CBC Weekend*. Among the people I interviewed were famed economist John Kenneth Galbraith and Paul Volcker, then undersecretary at the US treasury. My work ranged from the politics of the War Measures Act to meeting British Prime Minister Harold Wilson and Israel's Golda Meir, from a bikers' picnic to dinner parties with Roy Thomson and Malcolm Muggeridge. When a second weekly show was added to our responsibilities, Dick asked me to become the senior producer and line-up editor for this second edition to be shown midweek, called, surprisingly enough, *CBC Midweek.* My cup was full, and I was learning by doing.

In my travels, I tried to be budget-conscious. In summer 1969, I was asked to go to the UK to shoot a story on the ailing British economy. I was careful to ensure that the money I had been given would be devoted to what would be on screen. I arranged a cheap charter flight, slept on friends' floors, and generally was extremely thrifty. On my return, I submitted my expense account to Joe LeSaux, the man who supervised such business. The following day I was summoned to see Joe. I feared I must have spent more than I should. No, it was the reverse. Joe said that what I had submitted was not acceptable because it was so low that it would embarrass everyone else. I was told that such minimal expenses could never happen again. Spend more!

Let me tell you about my two most exciting nights on *CBC Weekend.*

The first was in October 1970. The Front de libération du Québec (FLQ) crisis was in full swing. James Cross had been kidnapped. And there were fears for the life of Quebec Deputy Premier Pierre Laporte who had also been seized. I had developed a relationship with British commentator Malcolm Muggeridge, who then had a popular series on BBC called *The Question Why*. Already conscious of the benefits of co-production, I had secured an agreement for Malcolm and the BBC to do an episode in Canada. Each week Malcolm took a theme which he phrased as a question: *Why Unions? Why War? Why Christianity?* And so on. He would gather in a studio a diversity of people interested in the subject and conduct a discussion, as only he could, to share with the audience perceptions, encourage them to think and make up their own mind. Given what was going on in Canada, the question was *Why Nationalism?* All shades of political opinion, Liberals, Conservatives, supporters of the FLQ, historians, immigrants, police officers, nuns, refugees, and the like were assembled in a studio in Ottawa.

Muggeridge was checked into the Chateau Laurier, but was then moved to a room on a special floor guarded by soldiers. The Quebec Premier Robert Bourassa had asked Prime Minister Trudeau to invoke the War Measures Act and to protect dignitaries from the risk of danger. Malcolm clearly fell into the category of those to be protected. The show, recorded on Saturday afternoon, went well and Malcolm departed for his flight back to London with the precious tape for transmission on BBC on Sunday. I did the same, flying back to Toronto where the half-hour Muggeridge show would become the main item on *CBC Weekend.* When I got back to the office just before midnight, we got wind that a body had been discovered in the trunk of a car in Saint Hubert near Montreal. It was then confirmed that it was Pierre Laporte. We had to begin again to plan a show that would clearly engage a huge audience. Contributors were assembled; Ideas exchanged throughout the night and into the early hours. I was directed to prepare shorter versions of *The Question Why?* at various lengths, as we knew there would be ongoing developments throughout Sunday: new reports, new guests, new stories. Eventually we went live to every time zone in Canada with a different and updated show, frequently re-editing segments for the next time zone as the show went out live in the current time zone. There is no high like live television and this was live television on steroids.

A similar "breaking news" situation occurred later that year when I was producing a Christmas edition of *CBC Weekend.*

The plan was to air a black-and-white film I had directed in Toronto and Newfoundland about two seminarians from the same class, one, Ken Bagnall, the editor of *The Globe Magazine*, the other a priest in the outport town of Twillingate, Newfoundland. This would be followed by the wonderful BBC film about Mother Teresa, *Something Beautiful for God*, hosted by Malcolm Muggeridge. No worries: a simple packaging job so most of the staff could be home for Christmas with their families. Then we heard that Michael Maclear's interviews with US prisoners of war in North Vietnam would be arriving that night. We had to open up the show to accommodate them, and we did not know whether Michael had five minutes of material or fifty minutes. My task was to cut versions of my film and the Mother Teresa film into various lengths to accommodate the news that would be arriving. All the American networks were waiting for this material to be fed to us and then on to them. I was very proud of the final three-item show we produced. Current affairs television at its best.

After four years at the CBC, Dick and I had become very close. I would be invited to dinner at his home with his wife Donna, their three daughters Camilla, Petrea, and Marta, and two Basenjis, barkless African dogs. Jenny and I would often go out with Dick and Donna on Friday or Saturday evening. In many ways Dick was a second father to me and I was the son he never had. We shared many approaches to life and ideas and I learned enormously from him. And he trusted me to deliver whatever he wanted. A former union organizer, Dick knew that he would never get any higher in the CBC bureaucracy: he was too opinionated and argumentative. Thus, we discussed ways in which we might both escape Mother Corporation. We talked of writing a book together. But curiously, it was the relationship I had developed with Malcolm

Muggeridge that sparked the series idea that would enable us to make our leap to freedom.

Malcolm Muggeridge was not just an English phenomenon; he had global appeal. A man of the world, he had lived large across several careers as a teacher, writer, journalist, spy, editor, and social commentator. His quick wit had made him a desirable guest on talk shows on both sides of the Atlantic. He was a controversialist. I was familiar with Muggeridge's appearances *on BBC Panorama* and the controversies he had stirred up over his career. When he was editor of *Punch* in the 1950s, he had written on the "Royal soap opera" (he was the first to use the term) and was vilified for it. As he grew older, his interests became more spiritual and he was often mocked as "St. Mugg" for this change of heart. From being a youthful socialist, he was quickly becoming known for taking on more conservative positions vis-à-vis the Rolling Stones (in tandem with the Archbishop of Canterbury) and Monty Python.

When searching for new segments for *CBC Weekend*, I had recalled a brilliant dinner party which the BBC had recorded hosted by Peter Ustinov. Good conversation, witty repartee, ideas abounding. I suggested to Dick that we should do something similar. We decided to pilot two such dinner parties, one with Canada's Lord Thomson of Fleet, publisher of *The Times*; the other with Malcolm Muggeridge. What a contrast. Lord Thomson saw this as a chance to show off his British establishment credentials, staging the dinner party in the Dorchester Hotel with guests such as Sir Dennis Hamilton and Angus Ogilvy, husband of Princess Alexandra. The most interesting item was my interview with the chef before the meal. Thomson was notoriously mean, and when I met with him before the dinner he asked where he should send the Dorchester bill. I said he should send it to himself as our contract specified that his modest fee would also cover the costs of the dinner. He immediately demanded that his secretary produce the contract, which he had obviously signed without reading carefully enough, and sure enough the deal was as I had represented it. He was not happy.

Malcolm, on the other hand, said that he would simply have the dinner at home and invite the neighbours in. That worried me. But what neighbours! Lord Longford, politician and social reformer; his wife historian Elizabeth Longford; Richard Ingrams, editor of the satirical magazine *Private Eye*; his wife Mary; and Malcolm's indominable wife Kitty, herself an elegant writer. Their conversation was sparkling, as exciting as the Thomson dinner had been dull. As I had done at the Dorchester, I interviewed the chef, who told me where she had purchased her ingredients … at the grocer's shop in Robertsbridge. The logistics of getting a four-camera mobile video truck into deepest rural Sussex was our greatest challenge, but this experience began a long relationship with Malcolm.

While I was away shooting, Dick had been reading Malcolm's latest book *Jesus Rediscovered*, and had the insight of taking the major thinkers whom Muggeridge referenced and making it the basis of a television series. Dick had the great idea of calling the project *A Third Testament*. The Old Testament and the New Testament were over two thousand years old. What would be the divinely inspired books of a "third" testament? This concept would let Malcolm expound on his favourite themes as we documented his heroes of the last two millennia. Eventually *A Third Testament* would include St. Augustine of Hippo, French scientist Blaise Pascal, British mystic and poet William Blake, Danish philosopher Soren Kierkegaard, Russian novelist Leo Tolstoy, and German theologian Dietrich Bonhoeffer, part of the failed plot to assassinate Hitler. Later I also directed a film that continued the series on Russian novelist Feodor Dostoevsky, another Muggeridge hero.

I will leave working with Malcolm and his idiosyncracies to the next chapter, but now we had a project and, if we could finance it, we could indeed escape the CBC. Eventually, after much persuasion, the CBC offered to pay one-third of the cost; I think they were keen to get rid of Dick. Its French-language counterpart, Société Radio-Canada, paid one-sixth; Muggeridge assured us he spoke good French, although, as it turned out, his French was on a par with Maurice Chevalier's English. Through contacts at Time-Life Films in New York, we secured a further third of the money; and the final piece came from a sponsorship with Noranda Mines, with whose CEO we had formed a strong relationship.

During the final year of *CBC Weekend* and *CBC Midweek*, Dick and I moonlighted writing proposals for *A Third Testament*, preparing the ground to finance our escape, with help from Anne Emin and the CBC's mimeograph machines. Little did Dick and I know that we would be jumping from the frying pan into a much more intense fire. But we would be free at last and Nielsen-Ferns Limited had its first project.

PART TWO

NIELSEN-FERNS

CHAPTER 4

INDEPENDENCE (1972–1976)

THE INDUSTRY INTO WHICH Dick and I emerged in 1972 as fledgling independent producers was not much of an industry for film or television producers of any kind. The cards were seemingly stacked against all of us who toiled in this sector. Had I, aged twenty-seven, now joined a community of outsiders?

We had achieved the financing of a modest documentary series and gotten the CBC to "commission" it. But, in truth, the CBC did not see us as any part of its future now that we were independent. Indy filmmakers were commissioned to make "fillers," interstitials, or short films to play if there was any time to fill between programs. This is how Nelvana, one of Canada's leading animation companies, got its start. Michael Hirsh, Patrick Loubert and Clive Smith formed Nelvana to create short animated films for the CBC's Rena Krawagna. When the three filmmakers were asked by their mentor Don Haig (who ran an editing house called Film Arts) why they wanted to start a company, Michael Hirsh replied that they wanted "to get into the industry." Haig's brusque and accurate response was: "There is no industry." From the outset,

I perceived that independent producers were really dependent producers, underdogs who felt like victims in a system favouring the big media entities.

It is worth noting the historical differences in the development of a film industry and a television industry, as well as the differences between American television and its origins in most other countries. Cinema is inherently international, especially in the era of silent movies, where language was not a problem and Hollywood was happy to import foreign talent such as Greta Garbo, Sarah Bernhardt, Rudolph Valentino, and Charlie Chaplin. When sound came in, some silent stars made the transition and some did not, but by then America had achieved world leadership in movie production, and the production value of their films assured their dominant position. American films popularized American myths and influenced filmmaking round the world. Some have said that American dominance of world cinema came about because the United States was a nation of immigrants from every corner of the globe. Cinema has to reach such a broad range of tastes (and not necessarily the lowest common denominator) and Hollywood found a storytelling style accessible to all. Furthermore, the size of the US market was such that they could cover production costs at home and adjust their prices however they chose when selling in other countries.

In English Canada, movies struggled as they attempted to compete with the US Goliath. The few English-language Canadian films that were made came mostly from the National Film Board. French Canada was a different story. While dubbed American films were popular in Quebec, and French films were imported from France, the Francophone audience wanted to hear their own voice and came to create their own stars. There was hope for the growth of an indigenous Québécois movie industry, as recounted by Dr. Constance Dilley in her book *Cross-Currents*. For an account of the English Canadian motion picture scene, I recommend *Hollywood North* by Michael Spencer with Suzan Ayscough.

In contrast to the movies being international, television, like radio, is intensely local or even parochial. News, weather, and sports are the bedrock of radio and TV, and in both media, communicating in the language of the viewers is key. Through networking, radio and television can and did become national. In every country, the state controls the airwaves and scarce spectrum has to be licensed.

In most countries, state or national or public broadcasting organizations were the first on the scene. Not so in the USA: land of the free and home of the brave. Competition is at the essence of the American experiment and rapidly three competitive networks were in operation and making their own programs.

Once these networks had matured, the Federal Communications Commission implemented in 1970 its financial and syndication rules (or "Fin-Syn") mandating that networks purchase their scripted content (as opposed to news, weather, and sports) from outside producers. The combination of network fees and syndication revenue meant that American producers covered all their production costs and often made handsome profits in their domestic market. They could then add to their profitability by selling the shows on the international market. No surprise that they made the best shows with the highest production values and again confirmed their world leadership position.

In Canada, on the other hand, the only competition among broadcasters was in the acquisition of American entertainment programming during buying trips to Los Angeles. This had no impact whatsoever on independent production. When Dick and I were starting out trying to find sponsors for our independent work, our efforts were frowned on by the CBC Sales Department: we were treading on their turf. Corporate production was a possibility, except that the National Film Board had a near monopoly on government work.

Competition generally raises the quality of what a nation produces. The BBC is the mother of Public Service broadcasters, and it remains a beacon for what such organizations can achieve. But the BBC was enhanced once it faced competition from ITV in 1955, with private broadcast companies such as Granada producing comparable drama and popular programming across all genres. But a true independent production sector in the UK had to wait until 1982 with the creation of Channel 4, which allowed the indies to really flourish. As Channel 4's first chief executive, Jeremy Isaacs, wrote in his book *Storm Over 4* that broadcasting institutions in general were

> hierarchical, self-important, necessarily embodying an ethos that informed all their action and utterance, [licensed] by the state to fulfil a conformist and consensual role. Competing with each other in theory, in practice their output converged toward a norm. The institutions, unconsciously almost, schooled their staff to think safe and produce predictable work; bureaucracy lay heavy on them.

He could have been describing the CBC we had left.

After Dick and I had pre-sold *A Third Testament,* our plan was to take off for the UK to spend time with Malcolm Muggeridge and to start our location surveys. For this we would need some money. Armed with contracts worth $300,000, we marched into our bank and asked if we could borrow $10,000. The answer was no. It was explained to us that these were "conditional contracts," namely that we had to satisfy the contractors that we had met their requirements at each stage, at which time they would advance us money. What the bank refused to understand was that no broadcaster would give us all the money up-front; staged payments give the broadcasters the means to have influence. If they did not like a rough cut, they could ask us to make changes, but they would never withhold the funds due at that time. Still the bank did not comprehend. They knew nothing of the industry. The lawyers we talked to did not have experience with international contracts. The accountants were unsure. And so it went. Dick and I quickly learned that we would have to educate the "experts" instead of them advising us. Without working capital, we were spending most of our time trying to stay ahead of the bank. We wanted to be creative producers but we first had to learn to become resourceful entrepreneurs.

We thought we might be able to secure some funding by hooking up with an equally "green" independent operation in Montreal called InterVideo Inc. Founded by Jean Lebel and his partner Nicole Godin, they intended to produce programs using a new technology: one inch video tape. InterVideo's resident technical genius also managed to build a mobile video unit inside a Ford Econoline truck. This was the future … or at least it would be once the stability of the recording and editing functions were resolved. I recall a lot of talk about "time base correctors," a technique to reduce or eliminate errors caused by mechanical instability present in analog recordings on mechanical media. I don't think this was ever satisfactorily resolved for InterVideo. As a result, Jean and Nicole, though ahead of their time, were condemned to doing cheap volume production to try to pay the bills. On location they recorded (but could not edit) Roller Derby. In studio they produced cooking shows with Madame Benoît, five episodes a day.

We scrambled for work in Montreal, Toronto, and Ottawa. During elections, both provincial and federal, we found ourselves engaged by the Liberals, the Tories, the NDP, and the Parti Québécois, sometimes all at the same time. We pitched for government work and to stage the Lotto Canada draw, the climax of a variety show which went out simultaneously in French and English on different networks. The original programs in French and English incorporated culturally specific acts with appeal to one language group or the other, intercut with performers such as René Simard who bridged the two solitudes and appeared in both versions. As this was done live, with hosts in different cities who combined in their presentation, it was a sophisticated technical and creative challenge. We ended up in unison with the Lotto Canada draw announced triumphantly in both languages. We also produced a feature film in French (*René Simard au Japon*) which launched spectacularly in the midst of a transit strike in Montreal. Box office receipts started strongly but rapidly declined as distances to a local theatre became a more daunting journey on foot.

Our association with InterVideo was fraught, as we had simply combined our cash flow problems. Jean and Nicole were delightful people and Dick and I wanted to help. Dick found an investor named Percy Bishop who dealt mainly in penny resource stocks to invest in both companies. He had made his money on the basis of one sound insight: buy land between the centre of a city and its airport. He owned an important plot of land in Etobicoke between downtown Toronto and the airport in Malton, now the

Lester B. Pearson International Airport. On Burnhamthorpe Road he had built two office towers. Though he did have money, he was loath to release it and, as we discovered, from time to time he too had cash flow problems of his own.

Our liaison with Percy was through Michael Murray. Michael's mother had worked for Percy and her son was brought up in the Bishop clan. I never asked if Percy was Michael's father, but there was a distinct physical resemblance. Michael lived in part of a Mississauga mansion owned by Percy's acknowledged son. Percy did not like the Bay Street establishment, and I had some sympathy, as one of my pieces on *CBC Weekend* had skewered that same establishment in an exposé of Bernie Cornfeld, the mutual funds fraudster. But now life with the Bishops and InterVideo made for a complicated and demanding business life.

Having left the embrace of Mother Corporation, our priority was to get *A Third Testament* into production. It was decided that I would spend the next year in the UK, based in London, while Dick would manage things at home. We had rented a small office at 38 Yorkville, filled with my furniture. By the time I returned a year later, our office would be housed more economically in Dick's basement, which is where I stayed on my sorties back to Canada.

Jenny and I had a great year in London, living in Lexham Gardens in Kensington (really in Earl's Court, affectionately known as Kangaroo Valley due to the many Australians who lived there). Jenny, who had had her fill of teaching, spent the year working for me on the series. That persuaded her that she did not want to work in the film industry either, and that if we were to have children, she would be a stay-at-home mom until the kids were in school. But the Canadian dollar was strong and we enjoyed all that London had to offer. I purchased a car for our location surveys, a brown Ford Cortina station wagon with a registration plate that included the letters DOG, which we dubbed our faithful "brown dog." And I had to buy a truck for the production unit, fitted out to accommodate all the equipment our cameraman and soundman would require.

Transportation was always an issue with Dick as he did not drive and initially would not fly. I drove him back and forth to New York while at the CBC, and I often drove him back and forth to Montreal in the InterVideo years. Now we were taking on the whole of Europe by road. Firstly, we had to get him to England. Dick booked his family to cross the Atlantic on a Polish ship, *TSS Stefan Batory*. I recall picking up the family at the docks and hearing that Canada had lost the first game in the Summit Series to the Soviets. Dick, an ardent hockey fan, was shocked.

We were all set to get down to work with Malcolm. But Malcolm as usual had taken on a number of other commitments, never knowing whether his television projects would come to fruition. I think he was surprised that we had pulled off the financing for a series whose ambitions were comparable to Sir Kenneth Clark's landmark series *Civilisation.* Though that series preceded ours, Muggeridge would say that "ours had the ideas left in." Sir Kenneth dealt with the externals of art and culture, while we were bound up with the interior of things, the spiritual and the eternal.

Our first meetings with Muggeridge in Robertsbridge revealed that Malcolm had no time available to write for us, so we would have to research and prepare everything ourselves. In our original list we had included the French philosopher, mystic, and political activist Simone Weil. Malcolm admitted that he had agreed to do a Simone Weil film with another producer. But his real preoccupation was completing the first volume of his magnificent autobiography *Chronicles of Wasted Time*. Thus, there was lots for us to do and we had very little access to our host.

Dick and I began our location tour driving to France for Blaise Pascal (but not Simone Weil), then on to Italy and Germany for Dietrich Bonhoeffer, then to Dick's second homeland Denmark for Soren Kierkegaard. We had hired director Jeremy Murray Brown, formerly with BBC's *Panorama*, to take on William Blake, and he would survey North Africa for St. Augustine. Dick was to direct the Pascal and Kierkegaard films, and would eventually involve Eric Frohn Nielsen (no relation) as his co-director. I would direct Bonhoeffer and Tolstoy. A location trip for Leo Tolstoy was not possible as the Soviets' only answer to our requests for access was "*nyet*." But all was not lost. Both Dick and I had Mitchell Sharp as our Member of Parliament back in Canada, and we appealed to him to see if the USSR might change its collective mind. Sharp was then Secretary of State for External Affairs and was in the midst of negotiating a massive wheat deal with the Russians. We must have become part of the deal. To our immense surprise "*nyet*" became "*da*." What the Soviets would not realize until we were already in the country was that this Canadian film crew making a film on Tolstoy would be bringing in Malcolm Muggeridge … and when they discovered that (too late to stop the film), there was a price to pay.

When he was asked why he had chosen these six individuals to be in his "Third Testament" pantheon, Muggeridge admitted in the introduction to the book of the series that it was only afterwards that he fully grasped the theme to which they all belonged.

> Previously, I had seen them singly and separately as six characters in search of God, and as such of great interest,

> and a formative influence in my own thinking and questing. Considering them as a group, it became clear to me that, although they were all quintessentially men of their time, they had a special role in common, which was none other than to relate their time to eternity… So, I came to see them as God's spies, posted in actual or potential enemy-occupied territory, the enemy being, of course, in this particular case, the Devil.

Muggeridge himself had been a spy during the Second World War. He concludes his introduction: "The first duty of stay-behind agents is to take on the coloration of the contemporary scene. One thing is certain though: whoever and wherever they may be, great services will be required of them and great dangers encompass them."

I will not dwell on the production of the series except to recount something from each of the two episodes I directed. Germany was a revelation to me: having grown up in England I had been inundated with the history of the Second World War. I was to discover Germany through the eyes of Dietrich Bonhoeffer, the theologian whose *Letters and Papers from Prison* is one of the greatest contemporary classics of Christian literature. He was in prison for his part in the plot to assassinate Hitler. Our first port of call was to visit his friend and biographer Eberhardt Bethge. We found him high up a mountain in Northern Italy taking a summer vacation. On the mountain in question there seemed to be Italians on the lesser slopes and only Germans above a certain altitude. Bethge was a treasure and through him I was able to uncover the only existing film footage of Bonhoeffer, home video shot in 8 mm in the back garden of the family home in Berlin.

We drove on to Austria, where we left Dick and his family to holiday. Jenny and I moved on to the Bonhoeffer ancestral home in Schwabisch Hall, and then journeyed to Flossenberg, the concentration camp where Bonhoeffer was executed. We found ourselves guessing at the ages of the proprietors of the small guest house where we stayed. Were they former Nazi prison guards? But the more time I spent in Germany and the more I met younger Germans, I found the place and the people open, welcoming and hospitable. Of course, there were some less so, like the old lady in Nuremberg Tourism Office who said there was nothing left of the grounds where the Nazi rallies had taken place. We found the site.

A complete contrast was Bethel, a settlement for the afflicted near the Westphalian town of Bielefeld, where we shared an open-air service surrounded by the so-called "useless lives" that were the target of the Nazi euthanasia laws. On to Berlin, a wonderful city, then divided by the brutal wall. We ventured into East Berlin via Checkpoint Charlie and found it a completely depressing experience. We were able to gain access to the prison where many of Bonhoeffer's letters were written to his young fiancée Maria von Wedermeyer. Maria's story of tracking Dietrich from prison to prison once Berlin was threatened by advancing Allied and Russian troops is completely heartrending. She would present herself at the gate of a concentration camp and ask if her fiancé was there. The guards would consult two lists (presumably the living and the recently dead) and say he was no longer there. On she went to the next camp. This was the love of her life and she never found him. When Malcolm interviewed Maria in her home in Boston, Massachusetts, she said,

> It was very hard to come to grips with the fact that this was indeed finished. I have continued to live my life looking at

> this as a great gift, a great … addition, a great enrichment of my life. Yet, on the other hand, it had its hard parts and it has been difficult, even to this very day, it is sometimes difficult to accept that it is no longer there. Nothing else has really quite replaced it.

A few years later, I heard that Maria had committed suicide, another victim of the Nazis.

The way Bonhoeffer's parents heard of his death was when they tuned into BBC Radio to hear a memorial service for their son, conducted in London by Bishop Bell. For the film we re-created the service with Bishop Trevor Huddleston reading Bell's sermon and a German choir (from a Lutheran Church in south London where Bonhoeffer had served) singing the same music. Bell concluded his address thus:

> So now Dietrich has gone. Our debt to him and to all others similarly murdered, is immense. He made the sacrifice of human prospects, of home, friends and career because he believed in God's vocation for his country, and refused to follow those false leaders who were the servants of the devil… The blood of the martyrs is the seed of the church.

Shooting *Tolstoy* in the USSR was one of the most intense experiences of my life. I came to make a number of films in the Soviet Union and it was never easy. Following the *Tolstoy* film, I directed a film on *Dostoevsky*, again with Malcom Muggeridge, produced a variety show in Russia hosted by Bruno Gerussi, co-produced with John McGreevy the *Peter Ustinov's Leningrad* episode for our

Cities series, and shot thirteen episodes of *Durrell in Russia*, a series on endangered species in the Soviet Union. After the collapse of the USSR, my company co-produced a four-hour drama mini-series *Young Catherine*, on the early life of Catherine the Great. This was a very different Russia where anything was possible; access to palaces, the Russian army as extras, etc. With the Soviets, the usual routine was to take me for a one-on-one dinner where there would be a bottle of wine and a bottle of vodka on the table. It was expected that both would be empty when we finished the meal. I developed a tolerance (or should I say capacity) for vodka. Next morning, we would negotiate. This usually involved me conceding more money to my hosts than in the original proposal, but I planned for this, so it was part of the game.

The Tolstoy negotiation was the most challenging, as it was the first. Malcolm and Kitty, our two-person film crew and I were greeted at the offices of Gostelradio in Moscow. The first question put aggressively to me was "Where is the sixth man?" I almost looked over my shoulder to see if one was coming, as I knew we were only five. I later realized that we had originally told Mitchell Sharp that it would be a three-man film crew. But with all the talk of the "third man" and the "fourth man" in speculation about the spy Kim Philby, it was unnerving to be asked about the "sixth man." Quickly they isolated me from the others and "negotiations" began. I was not prepared on this first occasion, but soon realized that this was a shake-down. I agreed to pay them some extra fees. This seemed to satisfy them. I was then introduced to my guide who conveniently did not speak English, but he had a very bright language student who became a vital link to reality. I explained to my guide that I would give him hard currency to pay for our accommodation and meals and would expect a receipt in return. Thus, my ass would be covered. I knew that he would exchange these funds on the black market and make himself a tidy profit. Thus, he would be cooperative. And it proved to be so.

Indeed, so happy were the team after the filming that they sent me a large 35-mm film can filled with caviar. Unfortunately, they did not seal it adequately, so it leaked. When the black-stained parcel was eventually delivered by Canada Post, it contained a note saying that it had been examined and approved by Canadian Customs. I doubt that Border Security would have such a sense of humour today.

The Russians wanted to see our scripts in advance. And we did not want to share them. We explained that Malcolm needed to experience a location and then he would write his script. They seemed to believe this despite the fact that when we arrived to film at a location, we already had elaborate cue cards in English and French for Malcolm to read from.

We were fortunate that our first shoot was at Tolstoy's graveside at his estate in Yasnaya Polyana. Tolstoy had chosen this place "on the edge of a ravine in the Zakaz forest; a ravine where, as his brother Nicholas used to say, a little green stick was hidden with the secret of universal love engraved on it." One of the Russian team, a woman who spoke English, clearly a Christian, broke into tears on hearing Malcolm's words. The officials did not know what to do or say, so we were allowed to continue. Eventually I realized that Malcolm could be a Christian propagandist on location in the Soviet Union as long as we did not defame the reputation of the great writer who was our subject; we could say what we wanted. We had secured freedom of speech despite all their efforts at control.

On day three of shooting, however, Moscow finally worked out who they had let into their country. Malcolm was the journalist who first revealed Stalin's crimes to the world: the famines, the executions, the slave labour camps in Siberia. Having become disillusioned by the West, Malcolm and Kitty had moved to the Soviet Union in the 1930s, but very quickly Malcolm saw that Stalin's great Communist Revolution was a sham. And he exposed it. I was summoned into a room by my guide who shouted at me for almost an hour that I had deceived the authorities; this performance was clearly for the benefit of the hidden microphones. He then took me outside into the garden and apologized.

The Soviets asked if they could interview Malcolm. We said yes. Then they asked to borrow our camera. We said yes. They said there would just be one question: why did Malcom admire Tolstoy? No problem. Then they suggested that Malcolm include a reference to Brezhnev's peace plan in the answer. I said he could not possibly do that! Still, they went ahead. What worried us was that whatever Malcolm said would be translated, and we would not be able to control that. This was the time when Aleksandr Solzhenitsyn was being persecuted by the Soviet state. Would they create some "fake news" for their own propaganda purposes?

The most poignant moment in our visit to Yasnaya Polyana was the day we asked to borrow a book from Tolstoy's library (all under lock and key) which Malcolm could use as a stage prop. He would be quoting a passage from Tolstoy and it would look better if his script was hidden in a book from which he appeared to be reading. The curator unlocked one of the bookcases and pulled out a volume at random. After we had shot the scene, our student translator asked if he could see the book. It was a pre-Revolution encyclopedia. Sergei disappeared behind a tree and I could see him frantically looking up passages. He knew what he wanted to find out about true Russian history. We left him to his "researches," but eventually I had to ask him to return the volume which in turn I gave to the curator to lock away. I felt bad that I was denying knowledge to my young friend, but that was the degree of control exerted by the state in Soviet Russia.

The final film included archive footage of Tolstoy's death and funeral as well as the scenes we shot in Moscow, on the estate and elsewhere. It was Malcolm's view that the novels of Tolstoy and Dostoevsky kept alive the Christian faith in the Soviet Union. Malcolm's peroration reads:

> Tolstoy's parables are the most artistically beautiful and powerful in their impact since the original ones in the New Testament. So, by a great twentieth-century miracle, the promise in the first chapter of the fourth gospel remains valid, even in the world's first overtly atheistic state. Thanks to Tolstoy, the Word goes on becoming flesh even there, full of grace and truth.

As a gesture to the Soviets, we had flown into Moscow on Aeroflot (never again!). We left on a Japanese Airlines flight to London. Greeted with warm towels, I relaxed into the realization that we had escaped with our film intact (though the Russians tried to have us process the film in Moscow). I had directed a complete one-hour documentary in two languages in two weeks, without screening any rushes. In many ways we had gone in blind and had got away with it.

Back in London, I called Jenny who had already returned to Toronto. She told me she had bought our first home in Toronto. We would reside there for the next twenty years.

CHAPTER 5

STRIVING AND SURVIVING

RETURNING TO CANADA IN 1973, I was immediately immersed in all the challenges of Nielsen-Ferns and InterVideo. We had to find enough business to keep ourselves solvent while we completed the post-production on *A Third Testament* and its French-language counterpart *Un Troisième Testament.* We produced *An Ark for Our Time,* an extraordinary film directed by Jeremy Murray Brown, about Jean Vanier's colony for the mentally challenged at L'Arche in France. The subjects of our film seemed strange and distant when we first encountered them, but thanks to the love and dedication of Vanier, his mother and their staff, by the end of the film we loved them all. Dick continued his relationship with Vanier, making a number of series and specials throughout his career after he and I had parted company.

One key relationship that helped us make ends meet was with the *Financial Post.* At *CBC Weekend* we had used FP contributor Clive Baxter on some of our economic reporting, and in due course we presented FP specials on relevant subjects. We saw value in marrying print and television, and over my career I have often had books created to parallel our TV series. Clive was very well-connected in Ottawa, and had a particularly good relationship with the Department of Industry, Trade and Commerce, whose departmental bureaucrats were growing increasingly frustrated with the National Film Board, which produced the bulk of the corporate films the government commissioned. They would frequently be sent an "NFB artiste" who wanted to follow their creative vision regardless of the film's purpose, its projected audience, or who was paying for the film. When we learned of their unhappiness, Dick and I devised a somewhat devious idea to help them achieve the results they desired.

The department wanted a film to promote Japanese tourism in Canada: a simple objective, but no matter what film the NFB might produce, it would never command any relevant distribution. I saw that we had to crack this distribution problem. I suggested that we should invite a well-known Japanese celebrity host to come to Canada. We would cover expenses for the host and a Japanese camera crew, and would secure access wherever they wanted to go. The risk was that they would have editorial control, but we felt confident that we could steer them in the right direction. The film ended up putting more emphasis on the Calgary Stampede and Niagara Falls than the department might have liked, but it was a film in Japanese with a *bona fide* Japanese star presenter. The show was telecast in prime time on Nippon TV, one of Japan's top private networks. The ratings went through the roof. Mission accomplished.

Unsurprisingly, the department wanted more such films: we had found a formula that worked. We proceeded with this model successfully in other countries, but the challenges became ever tougher. The department wanted a film for the UK whose aim was to reposition the image of Canadians as "hewers of wood and drawers of water." We were asked to show that Canada was more than a resource economy by demonstrating Canadian high technology. My solution was to approach the producers of *Tomorrow's World*, the top science and technology series in the UK, and offer to co-produce an episode in Canada. From the BBC's point of view, it was dealing with Nielsen-Ferns and didn't seem interested in knowing where our money was coming from. Had the BBC known it was the Canadian government, they would have run miles away. But we provided our share of the co-production costs, so this exotic episode was no more expensive for the BBC than shooting an episode back home in the UK. The BBC had editorial control, but we provided their producers with the research and all the access they needed. Everyone was happy, especially the department when they saw the ratings.

Finally, the request came for a show for the USA. This was the real challenge. The subject was the new Foreign Investment Review Agency that had been established to monitor American investment in Canadian industry. Our solution was to approach WNET, the New York public television station with whom we had co-produced the controversial Peter Pearson film for *Document*. We suggested a provocative title: *Canada: Not For Sale*. Not only was it a good show, it played on all 212 PBS stations across the continent, was deemed the highlight of the week and given a special repeat telecast. We had proved the notion that the private sector could do a better job than the National Film Board was proven … and would go on to prove it again.

After my year in London and our experience with *Tomorrow's World*, I thought co-production with the UK could be a major route to growth. The BBC's view of co-production was "you give us the money and we will make the programs." I suggested something a little different: co-producing one of their shows in a Canadian version. The reply I received from BBC executive Aubrey Singer was the rudest and most patronising message I had ever received. Why would the BBC want to have anything to do with a tiny company like ours? The next message I received from Singer was a couple of years later when he desperately wanted to acquire *A Third Testament* for BBC2. He had changed his tune. I would go on to have a productive co-production relationship with the BBC, both in documentaries with London (*Writers and Places, Tomorrow's World* and *The World about Us*), music programs with BBC Scotland, and both drama and documentaries with BBC Wales.

I returned to the USSR to direct Malcolm Muggeridge in the film *Dostoevsky*, very much in the tradition of *A Third Testament.* But this time the Russians knew what to expect. At our first meeting, they pointed to a pile of documents they had prepared on the great writer. It was about two feet tall. They insisted they had done all the research we needed. I thanked them and proceeded with the game of me conceding more money for their services. We left the meeting and never saw the pile of research documents ever again. We knew that our more controversial material needed to be shot in Moscow and the more familiar biographical material in Leningrad. But we had to shoot Moscow first. Malcolm preached Christianity and anti-Communism on the streets of Moscow, he denounced Lenin, and it seemed we were getting away with it. But punishment was waiting. When we arrived in Leningrad, we were assigned to a hotel under repair. There was no heat during the Russian winter, and no food. I had to line up each evening with Soviet citizens outside a supermarket where there was little to be had but bread and yogurt. This pleased Malcolm, the ascetic, but not my Canadian film crew. We found that the best hotel in Leningrad had a great buffet at lunchtime, so though we were losing a lot of valuable shooting time, we went there every day. This avoided a crew revolution.

I had the same guide as for the Tolstoy film, and we worked the same deal on paying for accommodation: I gave him hard currency and he gave me a receipt. But he became greedy. He wanted me to smuggle religious icons out of the country, sell them, and share the proceeds with him. I refused. If we were caught, Malcolm would be embarrassed on a global scale. On our final day, as we were leaving for the airport, I discovered that our cameraman was missing. He was not in his room; he was not outside loading the taxis; he was nowhere to be seen. Then I caught sight of him crossing the hotel lobby with a large package under his arm. The icons! I intercepted him and took the package. At the airport, after check-in, I sent the crew ahead to clear customs. I then beckoned to our guide, led him into the men's washroom and handed him the package. I simply said, "I believe these are yours," turned on my heel, and headed for customs. Again, the relief at clearing Soviet airspace was palpable.

Another important relationship for our fledgling company was with British naturalist and conservationist Gerald Durrell, well-known to British audiences for his amusing books about collecting animals and his efforts to breed endangered species in captivity for later release into the wild. He was to the UK what David Suzuki is to Canada. Dick and Jean Lebel had arranged to meet Gerry in Nimes, in the south of France, where Gerry's brother, writer

Lawrence Durrell of *The Alexandria Quartet* fame, had a home. As Gerry was fond of relating, he acknowledged that Lawrence was the better writer, but Gerry's books made a lot more money; *My Family and Other Animals* had been a bestseller. When we proposed making a documentary film about Gerry's conservation work, his response was simple. No. Lots of people wanted to make single documentaries about his work, but he was only interested in a series.

And that was the task I was set when Dick came home. A one-hour documentary might be produced for $100,000 at that time; a really good one would cost twice that. I came up with the concept for a thirteen-part series of half-hour programs to be shot on videotape rather than film for only $15,000 per episode. … We could deliver a thirteen-part series for $195,000, the price of a single quality documentary. And this is what we did, calling our series *The Stationary Ark*. TVOntario was our main broadcaster and the entire series was shot in Gerry's zoo in Jersey, including the birth of a gorilla.

Eventually I would produce four more series with Gerry, none as cheaply as the first. We took him with his new wife Lee to Mauritius and Madagascar for *Ark on the Move*; we co-produced a series with book publisher Dorling Kindersley called *The Amateur Naturalist*; we took him to the Soviet Union for *Durrell in Russia*; and finally co-produced *Ourselves and Other Animals* with another British partner, Jeremy Marre. All five series were screened on Channel Four, making Gerry their answer to the BBC's star presenter David Attenborough. My swansong with Gerry was a one-hour special for BBC called *Durrell's Ark* in which I interviewed Princess Anne in Buckingham Palace. She was the Patron of Durrell's Jersey Wildlife Preservation Trust. I was impressed by her, though the Palace was a dump.

Three more vital relationships were formed early in the life of Nielsen-Ferns Limited. All turned into friendships to last a lifetime. The first was with John McGreevy. Apocryphally, I heard that John was an orphan, found in Paddington Station, but in fact he was raised in an orphanage in Hampshire; later in life he discovered that his birth father had been a Canadian soldier killed in 1942 at Dieppe. He came to Canada as a young man and found a job in the mail room at the CBC. Rapidly rising through the ranks, John eventually became a producer at *Man Alive,* the CBC's religious slot, and once did a program with Malcolm Muggeridge for which he commissioned a set reminiscent of a monk's cell. This amused John greatly. John was an early independent director, but he did not want to create a company with an infrastructure; instead he successfully pursued an even more independent path with his wonderful partner Jennifer Puncher, the best production manager/line producer anyone could hope to have. Since John did not want to start his own production company, he needed Nielsen-Ferns Limited as a co-producing partner that would provide a measure of comfort to a broadcaster. It proved to be a reciprocal arrangement. We hired John as director for our film on Robertson Davies for BBC's series *Writers and Places,* and he and I continued working productively together throughout our respective careers.

John's big idea was *Cities*, a series of one-hour documentaries featuring famous performers, writers, or personalities who would introduce us to "their" city. "I have always been a lover of cities, finding in the passing parade on any street corner an inexhaustible source for reflection on the way we live," John wrote in his introduction to the book of the series. "So, the chance of visiting some of the great cities of the world in the company of gifted and highly articulate human beings was an opportunity not to be missed."

The first episode John shot was with psychiatrist R.D. Laing in Glasgow, but when he landed Peter Ustinov for Leningrad, the series started to sell itself. It was a club to which other famous people wished to belong. In due course, the members of the club included Anthony Burgess (*Rome*), Glenn Gould (*Toronto*), Germaine Greer (*Sydney*), John Huston (*Dublin*), Hildegard Knef (*Berlin*), Melina Mercouri (*Athens*), Jonathan Miller (*London*), George Plimpton (*New York*), Studs Terkel (*Chicago*), Elie Wiesel (*Jerusalem*), and Mai Zetterling (*Stockholm*). John and I later revisited this concept for another series of six episodes entitled *Return Journey* in the company of Omar Sharif (*Dr. Zhivago*), Susannah York (*Tom Jones*), Margot Kidder (*Superman*), Victor Banerjee (*A Passage to India*), operatic tenor Plácido Domingo, and country music star Wilf Carter.

The marriage of celebrity and intriguing locations has been the stuff of television for decades.

But John's stars were not just celebrities but people with something to say. We did not have to write their words: the narratives were lived experiences. When John approached Glenn Gould, Glenn had heard about the series and knew what John's request would be, except he was thinking we wanted the show to be about Orilla rather than Toronto. We had to point out that the series was called *Cities*!

The second enduring relationship that was nurtured at this time was with Karen Kain. Though I loved the theatre, I had never been a great fan of ballet. But a young first assistant director, Phil McPhedran, came to me with a proposal to make a film (his first) about this new star dancer who had just won a big award in Russia. He suggested I go see her perform with the National Ballet of Canada. It was love at first sight. This was a film I had to get made. At the time, Karen was due to tour Canada performing *Carmen* with the Ballet National de Marseille under choreographer Roland Petit. Apparently, the artistic director of the National Ballet of Canada, Alexander Grant, had been reluctant to give his permission for Karen to take this time away from the company, fearing that she would be tempted by offers from another country or another company. But the Ballet's Administrator Gerry Eldred prevailed over Grant's fears, saying that some freedom would be good for Karen's career and she would return home, as indeed proved to be the case. With the appointment of Erik Bruhn to succeed Grant, Karen could see a future in Canada and in the company, though naturally she was in great demand as a guest artist all over the world.

I sent McPhedran off to Marseilles to film rehearsals for *Carmen*. I gave him a list of things to shoot, including a bunch of picture postcards of Marseille. "Why?" asked Phil. I said he would find out in editing. His whole background had been in shooting drama from scripts, which gave him an eye for the performance sequences, but he knew nothing of how to construct a documentary and what it would require. I felt I was directing by remote control.

Back in Canada, we arranged shoots with Karen and her partner Frank Augustyn, with minimalist sets and costumes, filmed at the National Ballet School, with piano rather than orchestral accompaniment. The production value would come from the performance of *Carmen*, with full orchestra, sets, and costumes, in which Karen was magnificent.

It was only later in our work together that I had lengthy and complex rights negotiations with choreographers, set, costume and lighting designers, composers, conductors, musicians, dance companies, performers and, most difficult of all, stagehands, who were represented by the International Alliance of Theatrical Stage Employees (I.A.T.S.E.) I was to become the television advisor to the National Ballet of Canada and a Trustee of Canada's National Ballet School.

Karen Kain: Ballerina was the beginning of a series of documentaries and performances; our final production together was called *Karen Kain: Prima Ballerina.* In between these bookends, we made *Bold Steps* (co-produced with the BBC, which won the top prize at the prestigious Padua Arts Festival, full performances of *The Merry Widow, Alice,* and *La Ronde,* and excerpts from classics such as *The Sleeping Beauty, Swan Lake,* and *Romeo and Juliet* as well as contemporary work such as Roland Petit's *Proust* and Eliot Feld's *Echo.* We showcased Karen with some of her favourite partners including Rex Harrington, John Meehan, Denys Ganio, Serge Lavoie, Owen Montagu and, of course, Frank Augustyn.

Later on I also teamed up with Karen's husband Ross Petty to produce various pantomimes, some of which featured Karen. My newfound love affair with dance led to documentaries on prima ballerina Lynn Seymour and choreographer William Forsythe; full performances of *Onegin* and *Newcomers* with the National Ballet of Canada; *Swan Lake* with the English National Ballet starring Evelyn Hart; and *Big Top* with the Royal Winnipeg Ballet.

The third vital relationship was with the late Hagood Hardy. I was aware of *Hagood Hardy and The Montage* from seeing his group perform soon after returning to Canada. Like me, Hagood had come back to Canada in 1968. He was a jazz vibraphonist who played with Herbie Mann and George Shearing, and his group included a couple of female singers. It was easy listening. As it happened, Hagood lived next door to Imperial Oil executive Bob Landry, with whom we were discussing our first drama series. Hagood was enjoying success as a jingle composer and was shortly to release his hot single *The Homecoming*, based on a theme he wrote for a Salada Tea commercial. Hagood had ambitions to compose music for films lasting longer than thirty seconds, and I was seeking a composer for the film I had directed on *Dostoevsky* in which music would be crucial. This would give Hagood a chance to show what he could do.

I told Hagood that I wanted "poetry and jazz," a musical score that would enhance the drama and emotion but not fight with Malcolm's words. Hagood suggested a more classical approach that used high soprano voices and deep basses, which would leave Malcolm in the middle range for his commentary. Not only did this work, it created a peculiarly "Russian" feel, and I saw the further benefits of working with someone who had scored his filmed commercials to the exact frame.

This began a career for Hagood as a film composer that included *The Newcomers* for Nielsen Ferns, TV series such as Kevin Sullivan's *Anne of Green Gables* and *Anne of Avonlea,* and movies like *Second Wind* and *Klondike Fever.* One of my great pleasures was arranging for Hagood and his devoted wife Martha to spend a couple of months in Paris on the post-production of *Frontier*, working with a full symphony orchestra. They had the time of their lives.

During the initial period of building Nielsen-Ferns, hopes for independent producers were raised with the creation of the new private network Global Television, launched by Al Bruner in 1974 which we hoped would provide opportunities that the CBC and CTV did not. Despite their claim to have interest in those of us who worked in the independent sector, Global followed those outlets in doing much of its production in-house, and very quickly went bankrupt. It was purchased by Izzy Asper's CanWest and resuscitated, but it took several years before it could provide any help at all to independent producers.

In contrast, Canada at this time was developing the performing arts from coast to coast with astonishing success. Three major ballet companies (in Toronto, Montreal, and Winnipeg) were complemented by a wide range of impressive modern dance companies, no doubt due in part to Toronto and Winnipeg's fine ballet schools. Symphony orchestras in several provinces were getting better and better, attracting world-class musical directors and guest conductors. Theatre companies were springing up across the country to broaden the availability of new work by a plethora of exciting dramatists. Drawing from Rolf Hochhuth's and Peter Weiss' Theatre of Fact, Canada was developing its own documentary theatre tradition from John Gray's *Billy Bishop* and *18 Wheels,* to Paul Thompson's *The Farm Show* and the collective *Paper Wheat* to James Reaney's *The Donnelly Trilogy* and John Murrell's *Waiting for the Parade.* Robin Phillips had made The Stratford Festival a world class institution. Regional theatre was exciting. Canadian popular music was dominating our own airwaves. Comedy was thriving at Second City. But was this richness of talent appearing regularly on Canadian television or creating shows for it? Alas, no. This convinced me even more that Canada needed independent producers who could draw on this talent base and upgrade the entertainment options on Canadian-made television.

The first four years of Nielsen-Ferns and InterVideo taught me that when it comes to a collaborative enterprise like making television, relationships are paramount, and building those relationships requires trust, communication, and respect. But relationships were not enough. When Dick and I went into private business, we did many things right and a lot of things wrong. As personalities we were quite different, but we were both optimists and believed we could solve our problems through imagination. We thought we could sell our way out of our cash flow problems. Hence, we did not raise adequate working capital in order to be able to plan. We were always trying to raise money while sorting out which way to go. We were impressing those around us and winning awards, but we were yet to become good businessmen. At Nielsen-Ferns we were making modest profits; at InterVideo, we were losing money rather more rapidly.

While we all saw the two entities as being similar businesses, in reality we were very different. Nielsen-Ferns was a boutique Toronto-based production house working in the Canadian and international markets, while InterVideo was a Montreal-based facilities rental business, forced by lack of cash to focus mainly on the Quebec market. Thus, it was no surprise that when Torstar came looking at our operations in 1976, they were interested in Nielsen-Ferns but not in InterVideo.

How did Torstar become interested? Dick's brother Robert was a senior journalist at *The Toronto Star*, and much favoured by Beland Honderich, the newspaper's publisher. Torstar, the newspaper's parent company, had branched out to purchase Harlequin Enterprises, a publisher of romance novels. It was a brilliant acquisition that subsidized the newspaper for years. Part of the challenge the company faced was diversification, and the plan that Torstar had latched upon was the purchase of a broadcasting licence. It had eyes on buying Western Broadcasting.

Dick's brother was aware of the problems Dick and I were encountering in a marketplace that made little provision for the likes of us. He shared our predicament with Honderich, who invited Dick to a meeting at One Yonge Street. What Beland cannily saw was a relatively inexpensive way of acquiring some excellent window-dressing for Torstar's hoped-for appearance before the Canadian Radio-television and Telecommunications Commission (CRTC) which would be required to approve any purchase of Western Broadcasting.

Honderich agreed to have his development team, led by the impressive Roy Megarry, take a close look at Nielsen-Ferns and InterVideo. Despite their concerns about the latter, we had made it clear that the companies were bound together, and if Torstar wished to cherry-pick Nielsen-Ferns, they would have to "take care of" InterVideo. A deal was negotiated that helped Jean and Nicole manage their debt while Torstar purchased 90 percent of Nielsen-Ferns. Dick and I would each own 5 percent each of the company bearing our names. This seemed very attractive given our daily concerns about cash flow.

What neither side fully appreciated was that Dick and I had gone into business to make programs, while Torstar (surprise, surprise) was in business to make money. Their principal product, *The Toronto Star*, was sold daily for twenty-five cents a copy while Dick and I were engaged in an enterprise that required long periods of development, considerable investment and risk, and no guarantee of profitability. Dick and I had become masters of breaking even, and were always willing to put additional funds, even our fees, "on the screen" if we had to. The mismatch between our way of working and Torstar's meant that this did not turn out to be the marriage made in heaven that we had imagined.

CHAPTER 6

LIFE UNDER TORSTAR (1976–1981)

WHEN WE JOINED THE Torstar family in 1976, we found out they could be quite controlling in their insistence that we adhere to their rules. At that time, we had graduated from Dick's basement to offices downtown in the Regal Stationery Building on Wellington Street West, which housed our growing staff in a funky space in wood and canvas with plant boxes everywhere, appropriate to a boutique creative production house. The rock band Rough Trade rehearsed in warehouse space at the back of our offices. But this was not the look that Torstar wanted for its new "toy." They moved us to an office tower at 55 University Avenue and gave us an office designer whose work made us look like a very well-heeled insurance company. Immediately the industry thought that we were being richly supported and did not need the funds we still had to scramble for.

Another rule was that we could not produce anything unless it was fully funded. Often, we had raised financing for

90–95 percent of our budget which included a 15 percent production fee. We were not allowed to invest, even temporarily, a portion of our fees in order to get a production underway. Fortunately, Dick and I were bringing to the new company a slate of productions for which contracts had been signed and on which we could not renege. These included *Portraits of Power,* a twenty-six-part series co-produced with the *New York Times* (to be narrated by Henry Fonda), *Al Oeming: Man of the North*, a thirteen-part wildlife series, and commitments for our first drama series, to be shot in both English and French, the seven-hour *The Newcomers/Les Arrivants.* We were completing *Karen Kain: Ballerina* and a variety show, *Gerussi in Russia*, so we were very busy. And that work was keeping us in business while we jumped through hoops to get anything else off the ground.

The good side of the Torstar relationship, of which I took maximum advantage, was that we had a generous development fund and could travel to find partners and projects. This was how I came to lead the campaign to establish a world for independent television producers that would enable us and our colleagues to build sustainable businesses. I led a double life, developing Nielsen-Ferns business while at the same time lobbying for an independent's right to exist.

Thanks to the development fund, I was able to rapidly develop my British connections for co-productions, building on the relationship with the BBC and expanding to ITV, the network of regional commercial television franchises. Most other Canadian independents were trying to crack the US market, many looking south and then going south to join a huge Canadian diaspora in Hollywood. I preferred to look East to Europe and particularly the UK, as I "spoke the language" and, if patronized, could produce my

Cambridge credentials. My initial negotiation was with Yorkshire Television, where I had a long courtship, very nearly consummated with a couple of major mini-series, but never actually got over the finish line. However, in the process I learned much, both creatively and business-wise, from Yorkshire's executives, especially David Cunliffe, head of drama and Brian Harris, head of business affairs.

Our association with Torstar brought us some interest from British independent producers, of which there were very, very few; they most frequently had to work for BBC or ITV as freelance sub-contractors. We were approached by Irish producer James Mitchell, who told us that he had the rights to Lovat Dickson's book *Wilderness Man* and that Yorkshire Television was keen to proceed. The book told the amazing story of Grey Owl, probably the most famous "North American Indian" during the first half of the twentieth century, the writer and conservationist who saved beavers and proselytized on behalf of the environment, including a famous presentation at Buckingham Palace to the young Princesses Elizabeth and Margaret Rose. But the day after his death, it was revealed that he was actually Archie Belaney from Hastings, England, who played Cowboys and Indians as a child, wanted to become an Indian, which to the eyes of the world he did. What a great story, perfect for a Canadian/UK co-production.

We agreed a deal with James and off I went to Yorkshire Television in London. David Cunliffe explained that Yorkshire was indeed interested, but that James had not actually tied down the rights. Ever helpful, I asked our lawyers to help to finalize a deal, whereupon Cunliffe revealed that, after much internal deliberation, it would be better to buy out James as there were already too many cooks in the kitchen. So, having assisted James in securing the rights, we then paid him a bundle of money to exit the deal.

I later spent time with James, who became a good friend. I admired his later successes at Little Bird, his independent production company, which produced television series such as *The Irish RM* for Channel Four, and with his subsequent partner Jonathan Cavendish, movies such as *Bridget Jones' Diary* for Working Title.

The Grey Owl saga got even stranger when I was asked to meet Yorkshire's managing director Ward Thomas. He was happy to have a partner to share in the financing, and, though he was putting up the lion's share of the money, was content for Yorkshire to simply retain the UK rights, releasing to me all the international rights. Cunliffe and Harris were horrified to learn of this, but it was their boss who had made the deal!

We contracted the excellent British writer Alan Plater, who subsequently adapted *Barchester Chronicles* and *Fortunes of War*, two of my favourites. His screenplays for *Grey Owl* were terrific, but expensive to produce. Yorkshire's idea of a co-production was that we had to use their crews, even in Canada. These crews were heavily unionized, and the rules meant it would probably take a week just to get them from Leeds to Northern Ontario and ready for work. There were even stipulations to serve hot "bacon butties" to the crew at 11:00 a.m. each day on location. The costs became prohibitive and although we came within six weeks of starting production, the financing fell through. We had already chosen Ben Cross (*Chariots of Fire*) to play Belaney, over other auditioners such as Daniel Day-Lewis and Sam Shepard. For years I kept Ben's Grey Owl wig just in case our financing came through after all, but it did not get made.

For a time, we tried to pair *Grey Owl* with *Heaven on Earth*, a Margaret Atwood script on the "home children" exported to Canada by British philanthropic organizations when they realized they could not meet their goal of clearing British streets of orphans. (Australia got the convicts, Canada the orphans.) There was a CRTC provision that one could bundle (or "twin") two projects to achieve Canadian content status, and the financial help that went with it, on both as long as the package expended 50 percent on Canadian elements. Eventually we paired *Heaven on Earth* with another film and went looking for buyers; Atwood's orphans were rewritten several times to come from Yorkshire, then Glasgow (when we had a chance with BBC Scotland), and finally a coal mining village in South Wales for the eventual buyer, BBC Wales.

During our early years under Torstar, Dick was besieged by former colleagues, former rivals, and many new players to our acquaintance to join this seemingly "prosperous" new enterprise. Our management team was expanding and everyone who joined had eyes on becoming Dick's deputy. Colleagues wondered if I was worried about being usurped. I was not, as I did not wish to waste time on office politics. I had learned that success in television depends on trust and I knew I had Dick's. Besides, I had my eyes on a larger game of politics, the other half of my double life. Furthermore, while Dick liked to talk policies for the industry, he was not cut out to do the actual work of making change. He left this to me while he focused on surviving the challenges of Torstar.

Earlier in our partnership, I had suggested to Dick that we join the Canadian Film and Television Association. CFTA was a body representing the entrepreneurs who made up the "industry" in English-Canada. Its members consisted of laboratories and sound recording studios, people who rented equipment, and non-theatrical distributors. The producers were mainly small companies doing corporate or government work, and seemed unlikely to do much more. One exception was Budge Crawley from Ottawa. He was perhaps the first truly independent producer with aspirations with which I could identify. He was a rebel and had taken on the National Film Board. NFB had refused to acquire Budge and Judy Crawley's film *The Loon's Necklace*. The Crawleys' revenge came when the production won first prize at the Venice Film Festival. It also took the top prize at the first Canadian Film Awards. Imperial Oil eventually bought the film and gave it to the educational sector as part of their "good works."

Budge was proving that one could compete with the NFB, but his desire was to make feature films rather than documentaries. He succeeded in producing *The Luck of Ginger Coffey* in 1964 and *The Rowdyman* in 1971. Paradoxically, the films that did bring him global attention were theatrical documentaries: *Janis Joplin* in 1970, and *The Man Who Skied Down Everest* in 1975. However, this was not enough for the company to stave off bankruptcy. Budge was a pioneer, but perhaps more for himself than the industry. As his biographer Barbara Wade Rose wrote, "the loyalists at Crawley Films increasingly considered Budge not as a larger-than-life man who led them fearlessly into the future, but as a loose cannon with whom they had to cope."

Another renegade was Moses Znaimer. I was first aware of him as a host-contributor to the CBC's *Take Thirty,* and from pieces in the Toronto newspapers revealing that he slept in black silk sheets. He was a great self-promoter, which he used as a positive attribute for his various innovative projects, including CITY-TV. He combined intensely local news with movies and music videos, a potent formula for a younger demographic. He anticipated the rise of user-generated content by inviting the public to record their messages at his electronic Speakers' Corner. And he ran *The Baby*

Blue Movie in late night on the weekend: its soft-core pornography brought in good audience numbers, including American tourists who could watch pornography without shame and embarrassment in the privacy of a Toronto hotel room. My favourite initiative of his was a piece of interactive theatre called *Tamara*. Though Moses was a visionary and his studio designs were revolutionary, he was not part of the solution to the independent producers' problems. CITY-TV produced its original shows cheaply and in-house.

For many years the Canadian government had offered tax incentives in an attempt to kickstart the film industry, but without much success. There was a capital cost allowance of 60 percent which let investors write off this percentage of their investment. It had little effect. But in 1974 the rate was increased to 100 percent, which suddenly had appeal to high-income professionals who saw that they could write off their investments while only having to put up 20 percent of the amount being written off in the first year. Often, they were told that the films they invested in would make money and thus would provide a revenue stream to pay the other 80 percent as it became due over the next four years. It produced a bonanza for the industry, with the number of English-Canadian movies increasing from three in 1974 to seventy-seven in 1979, but the returns had been exaggerated and often what had been represented as a "get rich quick" investment turned into a short-term tax deferral and nothing more. The program also produced volume, but not quality. Some filmmakers made good films, but many more should never have been made at all. The most successful English-Canadian film of the era was Ted Kotcheff's *The Apprenticeship of Duddy Kravitz* (1974) based on Mordecai Richler's novel and with Richard Dreyfuss in the lead. In 1979, Ivan Reitman's *Meatballs* grossed $40 million on a $1.6 million budget.

But in 1981, the tax shelter bonanza was shut down, so another approach was needed to support a fledgling industry. We needed to learn from Québécois cinema, which mostly worked without tax shelters, but whose successful directors, such as Denys Arcand, Michel Brault, and Claude Jutra, had developed audience loyalties within that small market. They kept making films within realistic budgets, not inflated tax-shelter ones.

Nielsen-Ferns' engagement with tax shelter financing was a result of a relationship Dick had developed with Malcolm Matheson, a broker from Halifax. Malcolm saw the opportunity and seized it with both hands. My first dealings with Malcolm coincided with my first visit to the huge television market MIP-TV (*le marché international des programmes de télévision)* in Cannes. The company was supposed to be represented by Jim Hanley and Lyell Shields whom Dick had hired, but at the last minute both cried off and Dick told me to go in their stead and take along Malcolm Matheson with me to introduce him to the world of television. I was not a distributor, and knew nothing of that business. I was a planner who was not being given any time to plan. Normally a distributor takes months getting ready, organizing an exhibition where buyers can find you and watch samples of your work. None of that had been done, and the hotels in Cannes were all booked. But I was instructed to do the best I could. Instead of meeting me at Nice Airport, Malcolm, who had never been to Europe, flew to Toronto from Halifax so he could make the journey with me. I thought of us as two innocents embarking on a journey into the unknown.

We stayed the first night at the magnificent Negresco Hotel in nearby Nice, where we discovered the new rage: *la nouvelle cuisine.* I had read about it; Malcolm had never heard of it. The portions were miniscule and the bill astronomical. Malcolm felt cheated. The next morning we set off in our rented car following the coastline to Cannes. … Entering Cannes, we drove along the Croisette; Malcolm admired the Carlton Hotel and asked if we could stay there. "No," I responded, but later in our search, Malcolm got out of the car and went into the Carlton while I tried to solve the hotel dilemma. When I returned later, I discovered that Malcolm, who spoke no French, had spent his morning befriending the front desk, and he announced that he had "found" two rooms there. I don't know if money changed hands, but I accepted. This was the only time over the next thirty years that I stayed in the grandeur of the Carlton. By evening, Malcolm had found out the cost of the prostitutes lining a corridor off the lobby, not that I wanted to know. So much for two innocents.

I had to find out quickly how the market worked. I did a deal with Max Engel, a Canadian distributor, to share his stand and its cost. Somehow Max managed to use the stand for 90 percent of the time while I squeezed in meetings and screenings when I could. I thought I was looking at a significant sale to the Netherlands as several Dutch broadcasters requested screenings of one of our productions. I had half-a-dozen separate screenings for them and was confident there would be a bidding war. I told Max I was on to something when he explained that the Dutch referred their preferences to one central buyer who paid a standard price, so all my efforts were in vain.

One evening Malcolm and I went to a party in a villa outside the town. I got into various conversations and then discovered Malcolm contentedly sitting at a table. He told me he had just eaten the most wonderful soft cheese. I realized he must have consumed almost half a pound of unsalted butter. He did not surface the next day as he had to stay close to the toilet. And on it went, one adventure after another. We journeyed on to London where I had at least pre-arranged our modest hotel rooms. We journeyed back to Toronto together, and then it was on to Halifax for Malcolm.

Subsequently, I went to Halifax a couple of times to screen our work for Malcolm's investors. On the first occasion, it was a celebration. The second time, the questions were all about when the investors would see the returns they had clearly been promised. This was *not* how I wanted to finance our work. There had to be another way.

CHAPTER 7

MAKE OR BUY: THE CASE FOR INDEPENDENTS

SOON AFTER WE JOINED CFTA, I became the chair of CFTA's television division, and took the lead in creating a brief intervening in the application for the renewal of the CBC and Société Radio-Canada's network licences. Many of the arguments in the brief we prepared, dated September 1, 1978, helped to establish independent production at the CBC/SRC, and ultimately led to the creation of the Broadcast Program Development Fund of Telefilm Canada (then the CFDC). The document was accompanied by a 16-mm film entitled *Make or Buy: The Case for Independents.* In this effort, I was helped by Rupert Macnee (the son of actor Patrick Macnee) and Joan Schafer, then working for Moses Znaimer at CITY-TV. A report from the secretary of state in 1977 had encouraged the CBC to commission more work from Canada's private sector. In response, CBC President Al Johnson had stated that they would "make increasing use of the creative talents of independent Canadian producers. We must give more opportunity to independent producers across Canada to share in the national cultural heritage." Nice words, but only words. We wanted action.

Our short film presentation challenged the CBC and the National Film Board to open up to new talent and new ideas. Many of those seen on camera in the film had worked in one or both of these organizations and knew whereof they spoke. Dick Nielsen and I were prominent both for our work and in interviews, Dick revealing that Nielsen-Ferns had delivered $4.5 million in programming for which the CBC had paid a mere $225,000: no way to build a business. Budge Crawley and Moses Znaimer were forceful, as were a parade of independents. Pen Densham and John Watson told of the need to seek opportunity south of the border, which is where they ended up; John Lumby and Tom Fletcher, from Saskatchewan and Manitoba, respectively, spoke for the regional producers whose lot was even more dire than for those of us from Toronto and Montreal. It was a compelling presentation.

It is hard for members of an organization to see it clearly. During my four years at the CBC, I had not really perceived the extent of its troubles, nor thought much about how to address them. Now, as an independent producer, I could see that this was an organization in decline, badly led, and failing to fulfil its obligations as Canada's public broadcaster. Its defence was always that it lacked the funds it needed. This argument was compromised by the fact that unlike public television in other countries, the CBC was advertiser-supported. CBC management believed that there was no alternative to having commercials. But there was, and they refused to explore it. This dependence on advertising revenue compromised its role as a public service broadcaster and continues to do so. It causes them to copy the commercial networks, whose measure of success is purely ratings, instead of trying to be distinctive and different. What is important for a public broadcaster is the "reach" of its service, its ability to serve everyone some of the time. But the CBC's head was buried in the sand on this one.

None of the CBC's top twenty television programs were Canadian other than *Hockey Night in Canada*, and so it would substantially remain for the rest of the century. The CBC should have looked within its own organization to see why English television was so bad. Société Radio-Canada was a distinctive French-language television service because it found its own voice and created its own stars. English-language radio, which did not benefit from SRC's language protection, was still distinctive: twiddling the dial on your radio, you knew when you hit CBC Radio. The CBC claimed that competition from new services was eroding its audience, but its commercial rivals faced the very same challenges of declining audience shares, yet their decline was much, much less. The CBC prided itself on its news services, but commercial networks and private local stations alike were outperforming it in this area.

Part of the problem is that the CBC board of directors does not choose its president, the government does. In any event, the CBC board of directors is politically selected and for the most part perpetuates a lack of understanding of the business it is in. Governments usually select civil servants or lawyers to be the CBC president, or occasionally an engineer, but rarely does the president have any real media experience, let alone a creative or journalistic background. Small wonder that the organization has struggled. I have always maintained that governments have looked at the CBC as a large organization that needs to be managed, rather than a creative organization that needs to be led.

The Broadcasting Act "confirms the CBC's mandate as a national broadcaster, strengthens restrictions on foreign ownership, requires the predominant use of Canadian creators and talent, (and) reaffirms a vision of the broadcasting system as a means of strengthening Canada's cultural, social and economic structures." This definition was our starting point at CFTA in the ongoing struggle to build a viable independent production industry. At that point in time, the CBC did not, despite Al Johnson's words, really see the need for an independent sector and CTV did not even see the need for Canadian content programming at all. CTV would even appeal to the Supreme Court when the CRTC required it to produce thirteen hours of drama per year. Ours looked like an uphill struggle.

I had recognized by now that Canada had failed to build a sustainable feature film industry or loyal audience in English Canada despite all the funds being poured into the effort. Yes, we all went to the cinema, but to watch Hollywood films or the works of the great European directors. Much of the film "industry" looked down on television. But television was a more viable opportunity for independent producers, and there was a real and substantial audience out there for our work. The CBC, then, was to be our first target in trying to improve the situation for independents.

The CBC has four functions: as a carrier, a studio facilities company, a distributor, and as a producer. As a carrier we did not dispute the network's role as the nation's publisher, but that did not mean it had to be the producer of all its own programs. The vast majority of the CBC's scripted programming was produced in-house, but performed very poorly. Most of the acquired product came from the United States or to a lesser extent the United Kingdom. Meanwhile, independent producers like me had much better prospects to find commissions in the UK than in Canada as there were competitive outlets. We wanted the CBC to learn from the example of the United States and sub-contract its scripted shows to producers. Our argument was that an independent production sector would provide the necessary creative competition, improve quality, add diversity, save the CBC money, and deliver value to Canadian audiences.

The CBC had a roster of in-house producers who seemed to be there for life, and many of whom struggled to come up with one good idea, let alone ideas for the duration of a career. The analogy we made was to the book publishing industry: no self-respecting book publisher would put all its authors on staff regardless of whether they had one original idea to write or several. An author was as good as his or her last book, and it was the obligation of the publisher to produce the best books possible. All we independents asked for was a level playing field: a true marketplace for talent and ideas. As to the financial implications, outsourcing would shift risk away from the CBC and provide more value to the taxpayer.

The essence of the problem was that the CBC costed its programs using what they called direct and indirect dollars. We referred to them as real money and roubles. The indirect dollars were the charges for the facilities they owned and operated, often not that efficiently. The CBC would only consider paying for outside programs a portion of the direct dollars which they might use on one of their own productions. If CBC staff and facilities accounted for 80 percent of the costs of a CBC production, direct dollars might represent just 20 percent of a CBC program's overall budget.

So, in a CBC producer's mind, it was more "efficient" to produce in-house, as they did not really care how many roubles were expended on a production. This bred an ignorance of what a production actually costs and permitted massive inefficiency in how resources were used. At that time Canadian independent producers might recover 10 percent of their production costs from a sale to the CBC, which is not the foundation on which to build a sustainable industry.

Our brief asked the CBC for a commitment to $50 million during the licence renewal period, rising to 30 percent of programming funds within five years. Most observers thought we were asking for the moon.

What came next was the seminal idea. We proposed that in designating funds for the CBC, in addition to capital investment and operating expenses, "Parliament should earmark, in a 'third envelope,' a dollar commitment to independent production. Administration of these funds would remain within the province of the CBC." Our conclusion was that the private production sector was the logical source for a renewed and fulfilled Canadian Broadcasting Corporation. We had made the case, effectively I believe, but to our disappointment, the CBC's licences were renewed without the conditions we had asked for.

Early in 1978 I was appointed vice-president of CFTA under Fin Quinn, who ran a Toronto laboratory and sound facility. Labs, equipment houses, and distributors were the strong personalities in CFTA, plus a smattering of production houses doing corporate films. The big producers were actually small family businesses like Chetwynd Films, run by Sir Arthur Chetwynd and later his son Robin, or Ellis Enterprises, run by Ralph Ellis who would be succeeded by his son Stephen. This felt like a service industry, while new companies were launched by people who wanted to be creators and entrepreneurs. Nielsen-Ferns and Nelvana were among the first; others, in due course, included Atlantis Films, three students who formed a company led by Michael MacMillan; Insight Production Company, led by John Brunton; and Norfolk Communications, run by Bill Macadam…

Until our CBC intervention, CFTA seemed to me a relatively contented trade association administered by a part-time general manager John Teeter, who called the meetings and took the minutes. The Association had its own awards program and eventually Sir Arthur and Lady Chetwynd launched an Award for Entrepreneurial Excellence. Dick and I were its first recipients. The award was a wooden carving by a noted Québécois artist: ours was a beaver. Nelvana won the next year. Did they receive a moose? I cannot recall. In any event it was all very Canadian and low key. But the natives were getting restless. Bill Macadam of Norfolk Communications, Nelvana's Michael Hirsh, and I wanted to take on the broadcasters.

When Fin Quinn's lab ran into difficulties later in 1978, he stepped down and I was elected president of CFTA. I asked Bill Macadam to chair the Television Division, which he took on with enthusiasm and commitment. I was soon running crowded board meetings in the now palatially appointed board room of Nielsen-Ferns. And I was criss-crossing the country to promote our ideas. There were few statistics to prove our case, so I invented some numbers that were repeated so many times in speeches, interviews, and the like, by me and by others, that they came to be quoted as authoritative. All true except the facts!

The CRTC seemed to appreciate our arguments and declared that the CBC had to do better. The eventual result: the creation of a CBC department of independent production with CBC lawyer Roman Melnyk at its head. But ours was a Pyrrhic victory. The CBC was still not prepared to commit adequate funding for independent production. I kept articulating the "third envelope" idea to fund independent projects. The secretary of state's office had just introduced a points system for Canadian content, and I argued that if there was money set aside for independents to make some of that content, it could provide the building blocks for real change. But the idea would take time to percolate.

The points system was a response to the fact that despite the fiasco of the tax shelter boom, the certification of programs as Canadian was still essential, as the Department of Finance needed an objective measure if industry tax credits were to remain part of financing a production. The Income Tax Act requires specificity. Rules would also provide the guidelines for future funding initiatives, and to monitor the Canadian content quotas which broadcasters had to meet.

The CBC's definition was that anything they produced was Canadian content, while private broadcasters like CTV seemed to think that news, weather, and sports could satisfy their CanCon quota requirements if presented in a loose definition of prime time, while reserving entertainment programming for American content. Since this content was dumped cheaply on the Canadian market, a private broadcast licence was, in Lord Thomson's immortal words, "a license to print money." That was not good enough. Canadian broadcasters were getting away with delivering eyeballs by programming American content.

So how should one define "Canadian Content"? The points system was devised by two impressive women in the secretary of state's office, Dinah Hoyle and Andra Sheffer, to answer that question.

(Andra went on to have a pivotal role in the industry as the founding executive director of the Academy of Canadian Film and Television, where she launched the Genie Awards for feature films and the Gemini Awards for television.) As the president of CFTA, I was consulted by Dinah and Andra to approve their proposal, and then asked to "sell" the idea in speeches to and meetings with the industry, which I did, travelling from coast to coast.

To qualify as Canadian content under the points system, the producer must be a Canadian and must act as the central decision-maker from the development stage until the production is ready for commercial exploitation. The production must earn a minimum number of points out of ten based on key creative contributions. The writer and director each earned two points, the two leading on-screen performers earned one point each and the remaining four points were allocated to the production designer, the director of photography, the film editor, and the composer. One had to obtain at least six points out of a potential ten to be deemed Canadian. This provided flexibility, in particular regarding casting. One could have an American star as long as the production met the overall requirements. Additionally, 75 percent of the production's service costs must be paid to Canadians, and similarly at least 75 percent of the post-production costs. These were the broad strokes. In time, access to various funds required tighter definitions, but this was the starting point. Initially, certain programming genres were eligible and some were not.

Initially it had been the CRTC that certified Canadian status. In our early productions, all Nielsen-Ferns had to do was spend over 50 percent of the production costs on Canadian services. However, we were lured into strange subjective discussions, in particular when we used foreigners like Malcolm Muggeridge and Gerald Durrell as hosts. We were asked if *A Third Testament* was Canadian subject matter. We had to argue that while Christianity was not a specifically Canadian subject, it was clearly not a non-Canadian subject either. We were asked why we did not have a Canadian actor play Gerald Durrell. We explained that this was a documentary and we could not use actors. It was this kind of vagueness that encouraged both Canadians and potential foreign partners to believe that Canadian content was somehow defined by subject matter. It never was. What we at CFTA wanted was to encourage Canadian perspectives on subjects of universal audience appeal using Canadian storytellers. And we wanted to encourage the use of Canadian talent. The virtue of the points system was that it was objective. It focused on the use of Canadian creative and craft talent. The points system was a Canadian innovation, but it has since been taken up by jurisdictions all over the world.

As an alternative to meeting the points test, one could qualify as a co-production or co-venture, that is, a production funded by two or more countries in which the funding broadly matched the proportions of the production spending in each country, and that points were appropriately shared. In due course, one had to apply to Telefilm Canada for approval, as it had negotiated co-production treaties with numerous countries. These treaties now number more than sixty, some of which have never been used, but presumably required exotic trips for bureaucrats to negotiate them. Initially the ones with the UK and France were the ones most commonly used. Each treaty provides for a minimum contribution, frequently at least 20 percent or 30 percent from the minority partner.

The Department of Canadian Heritage (DCH) is now responsible for negotiating International Treaties and Memoranda of Understanding for co-productions. These treaties are administered by Telefilm Canada but ultimately require the approval of DCH. What these arrangements allow is for two or more countries to collaborate on a production in such a way as to permit each to enjoy the financial benefits available in their own country and to be granted national status. So, in the case of Canada, such a production could potentially secure federal and provincial tax credits as well as Canadian content status, making it more desirable to Canadian broadcasters who have to meet CanCon quotas. Also, such a television production might qualify for support from federal agencies such as CMF and equivalent provincial funds. For feature films, with Treaty status in hand, independent producers qualify for the higher level of tax credits for Canadian productions as opposed to the lower level for what are called Foreign Service tax credits. These latter encourage other countries, including the United States, to locate their productions in Canada, thus benefiting Canadian technical and craft workers.

Canada does not have a treaty with the United States. In fact, all its treaties are an effort to limit the pervasive influence of American storytelling. The US market has sufficient size to cover costs in its domestic market, whereas Canada and other countries around the world have to assemble enough resources to compete with this American dominance. International co-production treaties permit us to find budgets large enough to produce quality programs to combat American dominance and to protect alternative voices. In 2023–2024, the highest number of treaty co-productions were with France and the United Kingdom, followed by Belgium, Germany, and Ireland.

The treaties are important when one is using tax credit financing, which is now common. For this a new organization was created: the Canadian Audio-Visual Certification Office (CAVCO).

In our early days, Nielsen-Ferns was not making much use of tax shelters, and so we depended on the CRTC to certify us. One weird circumstance was a production called *Frontier* which I claimed as a majority Canadian co-production as our Canadian expenses were just over 50 percent. The French used a different exchange rate and claimed it as majority French as the total of the European funding and spending came to 50 percent. The British deemed this dramatic adventure series as "educational" and hence it qualified as a majority British production. *Frontier* had managed to achieve "domestic content" status in at least three national jurisdictions!

Documentaries could prove tricky. For example, if one was using a lot of archive film, one had to obtain at least 50 percent from Canadian sources. For our series *Portraits of Power* with the *New York Times*, we fortunately found an archive source in Ottawa that had a wealth of formerly German and British stock film, which meant we could meet the Canadian target. Gradually, order was being introduced to what had previously been a chaotic environment.

CHAPTER 8

THE NEWCOMERS/LES ARRIVANTS: COMING OF AGE

DURING THIS PERIOD OF politicking, Dick and I were working on potentially our most important production to date. We had heard that Imperial Oil was seeking a major project which would celebrate its hundredth anniversary in Canada. We approached their staff member responsible for the project, Gordon Hinch, a former CBC producer. Hinch said this was much too big for a little company like ours; Imperial Oil planned to approach the CBC and CTV, who would be given one year to come up with a suitable proposal. A year and a day later, we called Hinch to discover that CTV had not bothered to respond to his request and the CBC had sent over an idea for a religious series that had been delivered in an internal mail envelope tied with string. Was Hinch now willing to listen?

Nielsen-Ferns' idea was to create six dramas celebrating the immigrant experience in Canada, plus a prologue on the First Nations, set before "first contact." Both we and our sponsor wanted the best talent across Canada to contribute, and since neither Dick nor I were much impressed by the screenwriters then working in Canadian TV, we approached the best writers in Canada, whether novelists, playwrights, or poets. The list included Alice Munro, Timothy Findley, George Ryga, Al Purdy, Guy Fournier, and the like, who eagerly signed up to participate. They would work with Canada's best film directors and the finest actors.

Our concept for *The Newcomers/Les Arrivants* was to create a social history of Canada (a "people's history," if you will) that focused on those experiences common to all immigrants, regardless of time, nationality, or race, and on those periods in Canada's history when those experiences were most intensely realized. Themes included the constants of separation, prejudice, hardship, domestic conflict, homesickness, the search for freedom, and the crisis of identity. Our theme was that the land absorbs but does not homogenize newcomers. From the First Nations onward, each group makes its impact, each individual leaves their mark. No American "melting pot" for us, rather the brilliant mosaic that is Canada.

The series had to deliver on a number of fronts: it had to be both entertaining and educational; it had to be produced in both French and English, requiring original shooting in both languages (something Nielsen-Ferns did often, as much because it made good business sense as for the larger cultural purpose); and it had to be both representative and historically accurate. We appointed a distinguished board of historical advisers to help us.

Producing scripted drama was a challenge for me. I had never been to film school, did not have the creative experience, and had no technical knowledge; I had learned what I knew about documentary and factual production by osmosis, learning from camera operators and film editors, but I had never worked on this type of production before. To pursue a military analogy, I had joined the army as an officer, but had never gone through basic training, and now I was joining the navy as captain of the ship, but I had never been to sea.

My first time on a drama set was as producer for our prologue. We launched filming for the series in Hazelton in northern BC at the First Nations village of 'Ksan. Compounding my inexperience in the form, it was a hugely daunting exercise in a very remote location. Given the size of the crew and the amount of equipment, I soon saw that drama production required a military operation, organizing movement orders to get us from one location to another. Fortunately, we had a very experienced director, Eric Till, but quite properly, he was very demanding and let it be known that I, and the crew, had to shape up or ship out. I fired the first assistant director and promoted his second after an early disastrous day of screw-ups. The production improved and so did I.

Next year, our three episodes, about the French, the Scots, and the Irish, respectively, were filmed mainly in and around Mirabel Airport, plus Upper Canada Village. Mirabel was a perfect location, as the land had been expropriated to build the new international airport; we used the expropriated school as our production office and studio, and outside we found the geographic variety of Canada within a thirty-mile radius: coniferous forest, deciduous woodland, prairie, hills, and rivers. Fortunately, there was a lack of air traffic until late afternoon when the European flights started to arrive.

The following year of production was based in Ontario with location shoots both east and west. These films involved the waves of European settlement: Western Europeans (for which we told the story of Dick's family coming from Denmark to Plaster Rock, New Brunswick), Eastern Europeans (a Ukrainian story set in Saskatchewan), and Southern Europeans (an Italian story set in Toronto … and on location in Italy), with a marvellous elderly Italian couple played by Bruno Gerussi and Martha Henry.

Imperial Oil executives planned for the series to have specially conceived advertisements rather than conventional commercials. They did not adequately explain this plan to their president, Jack Armstrong, who announced at the media launch that there would be no commercials at all, just an Esso logo at the end of the credits. The executives were in fear of their leader and nobody corrected him then or later. And so it came to be. To compensate for the lack of commercials, we had to add an extra five minutes of drama to each film and were given no additional funding for our trouble. When Imperial's agency conducted surveys after the first telecasts on the CBC and Radio-Canada, they found widespread recognition of the series, but hardly any knowledge of Imperial Oil's association with it. That single Esso logo was not enough. But the show won us lots of awards and critical acclaim, including an Emmy nomination for the fourth episode. Not bad for a complete neophyte! Copies of *The Newcomers/Les Arrivants* were also donated to every school board in the country.

A less successful drama enterprise was our involvement in the second season of *The New Avengers. The Avengers* was a British series that ran in the UK from 1961 to 1969 and became a then-rare British success in the United States. Patrick Macnee played John Steed, an urbane gentleman spy in the mold of James Bond, and his female partner had been played by, successively, Honor Blackman, Diana Rigg, and a Canadian, Linda Thorson. The sustained popularity of the series in France led to a 1975 French television advertisement for Laurent Perrier champagne, in which Macnee and Thorson reprised their roles. The success of the commercials gave their producer, Rodolphe Roffi, the idea of rebooting the series as *The New Avengers*. Roffi persuaded Patrick Macnee to return, with two new partners, Mike Gambit (played by Gareth Hunt) and Purdey (played by Joanna Lumley). Twenty-six episodes were scheduled to be produced over two seasons, with financing from ITV in the UK and TF 1 in France, supported by the Rank Organization and Pinewood Studios. Roffi asked us to assist in the financing of the second set of thirteen episodes in exchange for the North American rights. We were also to produce the final four episodes in Toronto. This would really put us on the map. We got CTV on board in Canada and CBS south of the border.

In the midst of production, we were contacted by Roffi's UK and French partners to ask when they would receive their share of the proceeds of the sale to CBS. We asked them why, given that we held the North American rights and the associated revenues were ours. As it turned out, Roffi had also granted the North American rights to each of them. We learned that he had been badly over-budget and was using the money from the second series to pay off his debts from the first season. Our first indication that all was not right was when Patrick Macnee looked at his bank account and discovered he had not been paid. He angrily confronted us. Cleverly, Roffi had been paying Patrick's agent the commission due on Patrick's fees, so the agent assumed that his client was being paid at the same time. Though arrested in France, we were surprised to discover that Roffi did not end up in prison.

This experience left a bad taste in Torstar's mouth even though neither Dick nor I were at fault; Torstar had assigned us a young lawyer with no entertainment law experience, who had not realized we were dealing with a fraudster. Nielsen-Ferns' projected profits disappeared and Torstar demanded our shares in compensation. We were again employees rather than partners.

But we put a brave face on it. When we made a presentation to the Torstar corporate committee in August 1979, we pointed out that we had become Canada's largest independent producer of television programming, and that since Torstar had acquired the company, we had won eight major US awards plus an Emmy nomination, as well as numerous Canadian awards. In addition to *A Third Testament* and *The Newcomers/Les Arrivants*, we had produced *Hot Pops*, a variety series designed specifically to give Canadian performers exposure in the United States. In only two-and-a-half years since becoming part of Torstar, we had produced more drama than CTV, Global, and Canadian independent stations combined, and more bilingual programming than the CBC and Radio-Canada combined. Not a bad record to brag about, but we had to let our Torstar masters know that our market situation was dire.

"Nielsen Ferns has had to force its way into a marketplace which made no provision for its existence," we said. The CBC wanted to be sole producer of its Canadian productions; CTV drew its Canadian programming from its affiliates; and Global, as we put it, "has been permitted since its bankruptcy to renege on all its assurances to independent producers."

Our attempts to move forward ran into resistance from Torstar. One embarrassment came when we proposed to produce a series of romance movies based on the romance novel properties of Torstar's partner Harlequin Enterprises. What could be more natural? But Torstar told us we were not substantial enough to take this on. So we approached Harlequin's competitor Silhouette. They were interested and did not think we were too small to handle such a series. Torstar abruptly changed its mind and let us proceed with the Harlequin project. But we were well into production of the first movie when a small piece of our funding fell through. Given Torstar's strict rules about 100 percent financing, we had to close down production at a cost far greater than that piece of lost financing. This struck Dick and me as stunningly stupid.

Our next Gerald Durrell series, *Ark on the Move*, to be shot in Mauritius and Madagascar, required a final key piece of financing in order to meet Torstar's requirements, which I hoped to secure through co-production with the South African Broadcasting Corporation. I was scheduled to meet their representative Robin Knox Grant at the Monte Carlo Television Market. I arrived at the airport in Nice, where, over the years, I have lost more luggage than at any other airport in the world. My luggage did not arrive. I checked in at the Hotel de Paris opposite the famous casino and thought I should take a bath before my crucial meeting with SABC. The enormous bath had a device which could be used as a hand shower if one wished. I turned on the taps and suddenly this hand shower rose up like a python and drenched me from head to toe. I had no change of clothing, so I draped what I could over the radiators and hung my shirt over a lamp. The dinner hour approached and I kept checking the state of my clothes. The lamp had done a reasonable job on the body of the shirt but the arms were still wringing wet. I dressed and headed for the dining room where I was to make my pitch. I tried to be relaxed and charming, but it was hard when my shirt was clinging to my arms and I was hoping not to drip onto the table. Robin was delightful, my pitch was evidently good, and we were able to proceed with the series.

Throughout this period, I continued to devote a lot of time to CFTA and our lobbying efforts, as did Norfolk's Bill Macadam and Nelvana's Michael Hirsh, challenging the CBC to deal with us. Bill was a particular thorn in the CBC's side, eventually being blackballed for his vociferous and public criticism of its failures. The challenge to create a viable independent production industry, virtually from scratch, took enormous time and effort in addition to trying to survive and keep one's business alive. Bill was one of those who devoted his life to this crusade.

I had first met Bill when he approached *CBC Weekend* with *Their Mother's Sons*, a film he had shot at a motorcycle gang picnic, and Dick asked me to work with Bill to adapt a version suitable for national transmission. Bill was British, educated at Eton, and had come to Canada to become a bush pilot. He co-founded a regional airline and then moved to Ottawa to work for John Diefenbaker. Bill became vice president of the Conservative Party, running Robert Stanfield's campaign. He was fearless, as was evidenced by his celebrated CBC production *Connections: An Investigation of Organized Crime in Canada*, on which Dick served as executive producer. What emerged from the series was that the Canadian Mafia operated like much of Canadian industry as a subsidiary of larger American "enterprises." After a recent murder of a Mafia notable, Bill thought nothing of approaching another boss's limousine and knocking on its tinted windows to enquire whether the occupant would be running to be the new leader. When the program was telecast in June 1977 Bill watched the premiere at the hitmen's hangout in Hamilton. Asked whether this was dangerous, Bill reflected that any orders to have him disposed of would not be communicated that quickly. Bill went on to create Norfolk Communications combining excellent investigative journalism with a move into drama, his first series in that genre being *Jack London's Tales of the Klondike*.

Independent production companies like Nielsen-Ferns and Norfolk Communications were having an impact despite the CBC's inability to comprehend our plight or its own failures. Certainly, the CBC had no understanding of our circumstances. Bill Macadam told me that the CBC's Head of Independent Production did not know how tax shelters worked! Roman Melnyk apparently thought they provided 100 percent of the costs of production and the licence fees paid by the CBC were simply profits for the independent producer. A few years later, Bill explained to Melnyk that Channel Four in the UK paid a 100 percent commission plus a 15 percent fee to the independent producer. Melnyk refused to believe him. When Bill showed him the published terms of trade between Channel Four and the independent producers, Melnyk was gobsmacked.

I think Melnyk saw his role more as keeping us indy producers in our place rather than recognizing the potential of the CBC as a promoter and facilitator of industry growth. Indeed, Melnyk admitted in *Cinema Canada* that the most obvious difficulty for the independents was the CBC's primary obligation to its own creative departments. "If a department is planning a series on a certain topic, then the independents shouldn't expect us to be a market in that area." In other words, his job was more to protect the CBC rather than to promote independent production. So much for a level playing field!

I took aim at the CBC in May 1980 in a speech to the Canadian Cable Television Association at their annual convention in Vancouver. "Monopolies, particularly public ones, are the worst thing possible for the television viewer," I said. "Have you ever seen Soviet television? Or French television before it was split into three networks? Commercial television in Britain had an enormously healthy effect on the BBC. The problem with public monopolies is that they will never create popular programming. The CBC would never come up with *All in the Family*. It's too risky. It might offend against taste. It might fail ... whereas the news or a wildlife program or a ballet, even a bad ballet, you can't be criticized for programming that. Popular programming around the world has been dominated by Americans. Why? Money and competition."

Again, speaking to the Canadian Broadcasting League Conference: "The CBC is the only real program producer providing much beyond news, weather, sports and cheap forms of programming. Unfortunately, CBC programming is not popular programming." I went on: "In the mass media, quality is related to quantity. Public bodies and regulators don't seem to recognize this. They think we can survive with enlightened individual talents producing individual programs of high quality. What we must strive for is to put the talent of this country to work and keep it working because only out of such a creative environment will excellence emerge. We can't put producers in the position where they have one project and they must get it right or that is the end of them. They've got to feel they can take chances, that they can survive a failure or two."

The CBC was not the only Canadian institution with problems. In 1980, the National Film Board had a mission to China and the then Film Commissioner James De Beaujeu Domville decided to invite me, as president of CFTA, and Claude Godbout, president of CFTA's Quebec counterpart L'Association des Producteurs de Films de Quebec (APFQ). It was an amazing experience to see

China shortly after the devastations of the Cultural Revolution. We even travelled to Inner Mongolia and slept in the desert in a yurt and feasted on a barbecued lamb when the only utensil provided was a knife.

For Claude and me the highpoint was when we managed to separate Domville from his companions in a railway carriage compartment during a trip to The Great Wall. Armed with a bottle of whisky, our lengthy discussions led to his decision to hand over the bulk of government sponsored production to the independent sector. When Bill Litwak, his head of distribution (and strategic adviser) discovered this, he was furious, but for us it was an important victory, and another example of how much more effective we were when the French and English Canadian sectors worked in harmony.

I had already learned where the NFB's weak points lay from my experiences with the Department of Trade and Commerce, which had helped me to understand why the NFB had lost its way. It had once been home to many of the best feature film directors in Canada, both French-Canadian and English-Canadian, but things had gone wrong after the appointment of Sydney Newman as NFB Commissioner in 1970. Newman had done important work at the NFB early in his career, then at the CBC where he attracted talents such as Ted Kotcheff and Arthur Hailey. He moved to the UK in the 1960s where at ITV he created *Armchair Theatre* and subsequently as head of BBC Drama he launched *Dr. Who* and *The Forsythe Saga*. But what should have been a triumphal return to his native land proved to be a disaster. The unilingual Newman failed to inspire the French-Canadian creative community and fought with them instead. The English-Canadian feature film producers saw him as a "mere television man" and went off to fund their films haphazardly in the private sector. The obvious solution to the NFB's troubles was to do a long-term and encompassing deal with the CBC, but neither Newman nor the CBC could rise to the occasion, and Newman's contract was not renewed. A great opportunity for Canada was lost because the leadership of its then two prime cultural organizations could not get their acts together. Since that time, the NFB has been in steady decline.

Meanwhile, we tried to create breakthrough moments for independents. One such opportunity came in 1982 with the report of the Federal Cultural Policy Review Committee, created by a Liberal government and chaired by composer Louis Applebaum and writer/publisher Jacques Hebert, or "AppleBert" as they became known. What made all the difference for us was that AppleBert recommended that the CBC should give up producing its own programs in favour of giving the work to independents.

This provoked another discussion about the role and place of the CBC and a realization by the CBC that something had to change. The broadcaster attempted to solve the problem with the addition of a second channel, CBC-2/Tele-2. Independents welcomed the initial plans for the service, but when the application was published, the amounts set aside for commissioning independent productions were miniscule. Hence, we intervened to oppose the CBC's application with a brief entitled *More Is Less.* Our objections to the second CBC channel won the day, but, in retrospect, this is perhaps one of the industry policy questions which I fear I may have got wrong. New services necessarily have to establish themselves before they can offer the kind of licences we independents had hoped for. However, at the time, we felt we had been badly misled.

CHAPTER 9

PAY/CABLE: HOPE SPRINGS ETERNAL

THE NEXT BATTLE TO engage us was over pay television. Following a request from the federal Department of Communications in 1979, the CRTC had initiated an inquiry into the notion of pay television as a way to broaden the programming available to Canadian audiences. The Therrien Committee reported in 1980,and recommended that a more competitive industry be established. The department viewed Pay TV as a means of stimulating satellite usage and furthering the development of high technology industries. We saw it as our chance for recognition. Therrien's recommendations were accepted by both the government and the CRTC.

In preparation for the public discussion, the various producer associations had to come together. I only discovered while researching this book that it was the at the instigation of a "disinterested party" that unity of purpose was achieved. The woman in question was Elaine Waisglass, not entirely disinterested, as she was the wife of Nelvana's Michael Hirsh. Elaine was then a producer-researcher for CBC Radio and had attended the first Banff Television Festival in 1979. Listening in to the fears and complaints of the independent producers on various panels, she saw that their problems arose from the fact that the broadcasters made their own productions, and if pay television was to be a success for indys, this situation could not be repeated. Elaine found a CRTC representative at the festival who told her that if the producers wanted to prevent a cable industry takeover of programming and production, they had better get their act together.

I recall receiving an invitation from Elaine to a weekend meeting in the board room of the CFDC (The Canadian Film Development Corporation, later Telefilm Canada). CFTA could have two representatives, and Elaine made similar invitations to French Canada's APFQ, along with AMPIA (the Alberta Motion Picture Industry Association), to CAPA (the Canadian Animation Producers Association), led by Elaine's husband, and to CAMPP (the Canadian Association of Motion Picture Producers), which mostly represented line producers, production managers, and others in charge of production services on independent feature productions.

Elaine took minutes at the meeting, and she and a lawyer (Chalmers Adams, if I recall correctly, who had worked for both CFDC and Nielsen-Ferns) drafted the white paper that resulted. Elaine asked each association to contribute modest funds to this new Independent Producers Committee for Pay Television. This covered the costs of producing the document that was created. Elaine's work was done and she went back to producing radio. An angel had come among us and we did not realize just how important she was. What a selfless contribution to our cause!

As the leader of the largest of these associations, the next moves fell into my lap. Collectively, the independent production sector could now articulate our common aspirations for subscription television and the values we hoped the authorities would follow when licensing Pay Television.

We claimed to represent over 400 companies who had generated more than $200 million in production volume in 1979. We pointed out that we were responsible for more programming than all the private broadcasters put together. "Television is Canadian, it seems to us, when the experience to be shared is created by Canadians for Canadians," we said in proposing a model for Pay TV. Our belief was that creative competition was healthy. And if the audience is expected to pay for a service, it should be distinctive and different to commercial broadcasting, free from advertising and offering high quality.

Given the fact that the operators of these services would be competing for the consumers' discretionary dollars, we argued, producing the shows was properly the business of the private sector. Most importantly, we asked for a separation of the components of the system. The production industry, the programmer, and the delivery system must be separate from each other both as to ownership and as to operation. We were asserting that the production sector would be truly independent and could supply the needs of the licenced programmers.

We were convinced that the marketing of these services should not be pay per play but rather pay per package, with consumers paying by the month for a package of programs. In this new world, the measurement of Canadian content should be based on dollars spent. We urged that regulation should encourage an emphasis on increasing Canadian content rather than on restricting foreign content. Commercial broadcasters had long spent their money on foreign product and filled out their time requirements with cheap Canadian product. Our proposal was to increase the amount of money spent on Canadian productions and thereby keep the programmers honest. To be profitable, these programs would have to be competitive in the international marketplace. This would help build a sustainable industry.

We argued for a change in how Canadian content was measured. Traditionally, it was measured relative to the time of day it aired. In the new system we wanted, the measure should be the production of original material across the whole schedule, and that the programmer should not favour foreign product. We also argued for Canadian programs of varied length, to ensure that innovative producers and specialized material should not be discouraged in favour of a diet of movies.

The brief advocated that the first carriers should be required to deliver a complete service, so that it would be the consumer who selects which services they wanted and not the common carriers. We proposed one federal carrier in English and one in French, and at least one provincially licenced programmer for each province, though provincial licencees could act in concert to provide a kind of alternative network (rather like ITV in the UK). More importantly, all licencees should be subject to ongoing and regular review and unsatisfactory performance should result in forfeiture of the licence.

While we had not yet won our battle with the broadcasters, we could at least stop the next generation of big media from taking away our meal ticket.

During this period, Nielsen-Ferns had been able to produce all the committed projects Dick and I had brought to the deal with

Torstar in 1976, but not much else. Our partnership fell apart when Torstar was tipped off by someone in the Royal Commission on Newspapers (aka the Kent Commission) that cross-ownership of newspapers and broadcasting enterprises would be frowned upon. Torstar's purchase of Western Broadcasting would not go forward, and so Nielsen-Ferns no longer had any value as window-dressing to make that purchase possible. Our days as a creature of Torstar were numbered.

One final production before Torstar dumped us was a feature film based on Timothy Findley's novel *The Wars*, directed by Robin Phillips from Findley's screenplay. This was a co-production with the National Film Board, which proved to be a nightmarish partner with inadequate technical talent for the task. We successively replaced almost all the crew they nominated with higher-quality professionals. *The Wars* starred Brent Carver, Martha Henry, and William Hutt, and featured music by Glenn Gould, his last creative work before his untimely death. A magnificent coming together of superb Canadian talent, and Dick's finest creative achievement.

When the axe fell in 1981, all our productions were retained by Torstar, and we were told we could no longer trade under our own names. That was that. We were out on our ear and had to start all over again.

Harry and Maureen

My First Official Portrait

My godfather: Leonard W. Brockington, Q.C., LL.D., first Chairman of the CBC

Boat drill on *RMS Aquitania* with Dad and his three sons (1949)

My first starring role in the King Edward's School production of George Bernard Shaw's *Androcles and the Lion*, (1957)

Two 'n' One at Cambridge, with Martin Baily and Diana Lubbock (1967)

Working with Malcolm Muggeridge on *A Third Testament* (1974)

With Dick Nielsen in our Wellington Street office (1975)

A gift from the star of *Karen Kain: Ballerina* (1975)

Glenn Gould in *Cities*. (1976) Glenn's last work before his untimely death was composing the score for *The Wars*

First recipients of the Chetwynd Award for Entrepreneurial Excellence, Dick and I receive a carving from Sir Arthur and Lady Chetwynd.

At a music recording with Hagood Hardy, composer for *Dostoevsky* (1976)

Dick and me in good times

Bill Macadam, Norfolk Communications and Chair, CFTA Television Division

Michael Hirsh, Nelvana and Co-President, ACFTP

The National Film Board of Canada delegation to China, including Pat Michel (2nd from left), me (3rd), Jim Domville (4th), Bill Litwak (6th) and Claude Godbout (10th) Apologies to our Chinese hosts and colleagues whose names have disappeared from my memory (1980)

Two "partners in crime" outside their yurt in Inner Mongolia: Claude Godbout (APFQ) and me (CFTA) during the visit to China (1980)

Recording narration for *Portraits of Power* with Henry Fonda (1977)

Judd Buchanan, Minister of Public Works, hands me the key to the expropriated school in Mirabel which was our base for the second year of production of *The Newcomers/Les Arrivants* (1978)

Launching *Hotpops* with the Canadian Recording Industry Association's President Brian Robertson, backed by a vanity wall of assorted awards (1979)

Accepting ACTRA's Nellie Award for the Best Television Program of the Year from Prime Minister Pierre Trudeau, with John Gray and Eric Peterson (1982)

At the National Arts Centre, working with Martha Henry on *Stage on Screen* (1991)

William Hutt, Martha Henry and Brent Carver in Timothy Findley's *The Wars*, directed by Robin Phillips (1981)

My children Andrew, Katharine and Mark, dressed for Hallowe'en with Gerry and Lee Durrell in *The Amateur Naturalist* (1983)

Andrew and Katharine as orphans with me as the Sea Captain in Margaret Atwood's *Heaven On Earth*, directed by Allan Kroeker (1987)

Poster promoting *Heaven on Earth*, Canada's first production on PBS' *Masterpiece Theatre* (1986)

RH Thomson as Frederick Banting, Canada's first Nobel prizewinner, in *Glory Enough for All*, directed by Eric Till (1988)

The first print of folk artist Linda Evans's rendition of A Decade of Excellence at the Banff Television Festival, presented to me "for five years of outstanding leadership" at the 10th anniversary and the conclusion of my term as Chair of the Festival's Board of Directors (1989)

A year's worth of Banff events around the world. (2003–2004)

A gathering of Presidents at Banff: Pierre Juneau (CBC), me (Banff Television Foundation) and Murray Chercover (CTV) (1989)

British producer Paul Jackson pitches at the Banff Market Simulation and I seek reaction from panelists Patrick Dromgoole (UK), Jacques Dercourt (France), Norman Horowitz (USA) and Richard Price (UK) (1989)

Dining with Jane Fonda at Banff when her then husband Ted Turner won the Outstanding Achievement Award (1991)

Walter Cronkite and Sir Peter Ustinov with Carrie Hunter at Banff (1991)

With Bob Newhart

With John Candy

With Steve Smith (*Red Green*) before the Banff Western Barbecue

The Who's Roger Daltrey as William Dampier in *Pirate Tales* (1995)

Captain Cook: Obsession and Discovery (2007)

With my family at the presentation of my Academy Lifetime Achievement Award (2000)

Receiving the Order of Canada from Governor General Michaëlle Jean (2006)

With Orna Yarmut at CoPro (2018)

Me, in action.

With Ruby Chen at CCDF

"O to be young again!"

PART THREE

PRIMEDIA

CHAPTER 10

FREE AGAIN—AND HOPES DASHED (1981–1985)

DICK AND I FOUND new premises on Front Street East opposite the offices and plant of *The Toronto Sun*. We had the top floor of an old factory which was reached after climbing three intimidating flights of stairs on one side of the building. We hung out our new shingle, Primedia Productions, and Dick worked both on completing *The Wars* and writing screenplays to work through his frustrations. The Toronto International Film Festival wanted to give *The Wars* its world premiere as its opening offering, but this was vetoed by Beland Honderich. A public screening might have reduced Torstar's flexibility as to which year they could expense the movie's costs which might have had tax consequences. As ever, business trumped art.

My task was to find new productions and co-productions and to continue the work of industry building. Having led the way in the development of the industry, Dick and I now found ourselves lagging behind the emerging players such as Alliance, Atlantis, Nelvana, and a plethora of French-Canadian companies.

While in February 1980 the Independent Producers Committee for Pay Television had been speaking with one voice, a year later the potential impact of this new "hope" had stirred up dissention among the members of various industry associations. CFTA wanted to avoid internal strife, as a number of members were potential Pay TV applicants. Their fears led to caution, and this produced the result it had tried so hard to avoid. One voice became several, each speaking for self-interest rather than the good of the community. The infighting became intense between the television producers, the production service industry, and the feature film producers. Dick and I had alienated some within CFTA by recognizing that new Pay TV players would realistically want some security of supply if a large group of new producers came on the scene. We advocated for "core companies," executive producing companies who would mentor the less experienced and provide comfort to the broadcasters. We had already been doing this with some success with several regional producers or individual talents, but it was interpreted as an attempt to control others.

I stepped down as CFTA president in April 1982. I felt we needed a less restrictive lobbying platform to make the case for Canadian independent television. Breaking away from CFTA, a group of producers launched a new Association of Canadian Film and Television Producers (ACFTP), with Michael Hirsh and me as its co-presidents. We had felt that the old-established CFTA players had become a drag on our passion for a truly independent production sector, just as the Gang of Nine feature film producers had felt a drag from the non-entrepreneurial members of CAMPP. Rising hopes and dashed dreams led to continuing infighting among the television producers and the feature film producers. Individual producers were tying their fortunes to one licence applicant or another. On one occasion, in search of a truce between the warring factions, as co-president of ACFTP, I even forged a compact with Garth Drabinsky of the Gang of Nine only to be betrayed by him within the hour. What had happened to trust?

Suffice it to say, passions remained high, and these were increasingly intense and heady times. Alliances were being formed and then broken. The hearings for the new potential licencees saw producers align with one candidate or another, and competition for such support was aggressive.

At that time the CRTC was chaired by Dr. John Meisel, an amiable academic with little practical experience of the industry. He liked what he saw when he looked at the British television industry, particularly the structure of the main commercial network, ITV. It consisted of five large regional companies and another nine smaller regional licencees. The big players had their own production facilities producing the full range of output from drama to game shows. But that model was not possible in Canada. The differences were that the UK was twice the size of Canada in terms of population, and ITV's only competition was the BBC, not every broadcast network in North America.

In 1982 the CRTC announced its decisions: instead of two strong national services, it granted six competitive services: First Choice, the name of two national movie networks (in English and French); three regional general-interest channels; Star Channel in Atlantic Canada; SuperChannel in Ontario and Alberta; C-Channel, a performing arts service; and a regional multilingual service in B.C. Subsequently, even more regional channels were authorized. Time and revenue quotas were imposed to ensure Canadian programming, but much of how the companies would operate was left vague, and there were no terms of trade with the emerging independent production community. Similarly, the retail price to the subscriber was left unregulated.

In February 1983 these pay services became operational, and all hell broke loose.

First Choice, the national, general-interest licencee, announced a joint venture with an American production company whereby $30 million in "adult" films would be produced to help meet Canadian regulatory obligations. Meisel requested the industry to draw up guidelines for self-regulation. It soon became apparent that some licencees were fulfilling their programming obligations by flowing through preproduction revenues from US sources and counting these as Canadian production contributions for regulatory purposes. This was called "scaffolding." Everyone was trying to subvert the system in order to survive, as subscriptions were not meeting projections.

Star Channel eventually was shut down; a French-language regional service, TVEC, merged with First Choice, which was itself refinanced and taken over by a film production/distribution company. By 1987 only two of the original pay licences remained, each now afforded regional monopolies: First Choice had a monopoly east of Manitoba and SuperChannel had one in the West. It was only by packaging the movie channel with specialty services and eliminating direct competition that the pay industry finally began to turn a profit. Canada did not have the market size to handle the theoretical highly competitive model dreamed up by Meisel and the CRTC.

Pay TV was a radical departure from historic broadcasting policy. There was no role for the public sector. Market forces were allowed to run riot. Diversity and cultural objectives were seemingly given primacy … and then not. Advancing technological objectives was stressed. In all it was a hodge-podge of hopes untethered to reality.

The fastest collapse among the new networks was C-Channel, the arts network, which only lasted seventeen weeks. Primedia had sold the channel *The Country Classic*, a telecast of the first country music concert from the recently opened Roy Thomson Hall. Our financing involved a Pay TV window followed by deals with free TV broadcasters to run the show after the pay "window". I flamboyantly wore a tuxedo with a Stetson hat and cowboy boots to the event, after which we rushed to completion and sent over the tape. C-Channel took delivery, but the bailiffs had already closed the reception desk where our cheque was waiting. Then, in order to stave off its impending bankruptcy, C-Channel decided to run its programming for free, including *The Country Classic*, thereby nullifying our free TV licences. So not only did C-Channel fail to pay us, it denied us any other revenue from our prime market. Fortunately, our post-production house said we could pay back our substantial debt over time, which we did, but it meant we would not make any profits for the next couple of years.

Given our disappointments with Pay TV, we again turned our attention to the CBC and aggressively promoted my idea of a "third envelope." The CBC still claimed that there was no money for independent production, and 85 percent of prime-time programming on Canadian television came from abroad, mainly the United States. But in 1983, the federal government released the statement *Towards a New National Broadcasting Policy* and the following year Francis Fox, the Minister of Communications, issued his *National Film and Video Policy.* The policy was aimed at making the Canadian broadcasting system more competitive in the face of new technologies, and included the establishment of the Broadcast Program Development Fund administered by the Canadian Film Development Corporation (soon to be renamed Telefilm Canada to reflect this new commitment to television). There would now be an infusion of $35 million to fund independent film and television production. This could be transformative.

The government's policies for the motion picture industry had failed, at least as far as English Canada was concerned. By now including television in their incentives, both through tax credits and this new Telefilm Fund, we at last had a chance to connect with Canadian audiences, to have sustainable budgets, and to force the broadcasters to deal with us.

CBC President Al Johnson was furious about the new fund and resisted vehemently. He maintained that he would never allow anyone to share editorial decision-making with the CBC, ignoring the fact that fund required broadcaster approval before any funding would flow. The result of Johnson's intransigence was that instead of the CBC potentially being the sole beneficiary of this fund (as we had initially argued), the government determined that the money would now be shared with private sector broadcasters who were guaranteed access to at least half the fund.

Francis Fox was now persuaded that giving the CBC any privileged access to these funds would lead to them to squander a portion of it on fees for themselves and charges for their own services. And by not giving it exclusively for CBC productions, it now actively encouraged private broadcasters to commission Canadian entertainment product instead of just acquiring American productions. The Broadcast Program Development Fund was to become the prime instrument in building a viable and sustainable independent production sector. Though a public sector initiative, its very existence encouraged dilatory private broadcasters to start commissioning real, independently produced Canadian television: drama, variety, and documentary. Incentives work! And in time provincial governments followed suit.

By contrast, the fight for independent producers in the UK was very different to what we had faced in Canada. British television was not initially a competitive market place. When commercial television (ITV) was licensed in 1955 to compete with BBC, a monopoly simply became a duopoly. As in Canada, there would be a succession of commissions to guide policies regarding the future expansion of television. After a rocky start, ITV had come to command a 70:30 lead over the BBC in audience ratings, a situation that the Pilkington Report was to address in recommending a third channel. The BBC saw that it had to throw off some of its bureaucratic ways and embrace a broader range of talent. They prepared well; their clear aim was to redress this audience imbalance. The ITV companies, somewhat complacent in their success, took a beating. The recommendation in 1962 was that BBC be given a second channel, BBC-2.

Fifteen years later, another Commission, the Annan Committee, reported in 1977. ITV was praised, but did not get the prize they had been hoping for: ITV-2 to parallel BBC-2. Annan recommended that the fourth channel be run by a separate authority, an Open Broadcast Authority, which would oversee a "channel publishing other people's ideas" rather than relying on an internal staff to produce its programs. This put the cat among the pigeons.

ITV was outraged as were the unions who saw a threat to jobs within ITV. It all came to a head at the 1977 Edinburgh International Television Festival which had become a great talkfest. Its opening keynote lecture was given by the great French documentarian Marcel Ophuls (*The Sorrow and the Pity*). He attacked the unimaginative puritans who seemed to run television. He was followed by British writer Dennis Potter whose *Brimstone and Treacle* had been banned by BBC. Potter took the BBC leadership to task: the natives were getting restless. Jeremy Isaacs, Director of Programmes at Thames Television, who had been responsible for such courageous films as *The Naked Civil Servant* and *Rock Follies*, seized the moment and urged that a letter of protest should be sent to the chairman of the BBC. This eruption caused uproar in the media and transformed the festival into a key platform for discussion of the policy for the media.

Annan's report led to a white paper on broadcasting, published the next year in time for the next edition of the Edinburgh International Television Festival. By then the independent producers had formed a Channel Four Group to lobby for its interests. But time was running out. An election was expected by the following October. However, the government did confirm it was proposing a channel that would "explore the possibilities of programmes which say something new in new ways. The aim will be to widen the choice available to viewers … and not intended to compete with programmes on existing channels." In the House of Commons, William Whitelaw agreed with this aim, but not the creation of a new authority as Annan had suggested.

With the election of Margaret Thatcher in May 1979, it was feared that everything that had been lobbied for would be lost. The campaigners realized that Edinburgh 1979 would be their last chance to influence whatever the government might legislate. *TV-4 The Case for Independence*, a thirteen-page position paper, was circulated. Jeremy Isaacs was scheduled to give the MacTaggart Lecture. This was the perfect platform from which to set out his vision. Cleverly, he began by defending ITV and arguing powerfully that BBC should be properly funded. He then proposed that the new channel neither simply compete with ITV nor be merely complementary to it. His prescription: a channel that everyone will watch some of the time and no-one will watch all of the time. But he stressed that the leadership of the channel had to be independent of the ITV companies, though they could be represented on the Board. The channel would be funded by a levy on these ITV companies, but they would sell the advertising for the channel. His target audience for the new service: 10 percent.

Isaacs was realistic about the emerging independent sector. He proposed a minimum guarantee for programs that it would supply as opposed to programs from the ITV companies and that this would grow as need and merit would determine. Channel Four would not employ any producers. But its commissioning editors would decide what they wanted: there was no automatic right for indys to be programmed on the channel. Genuine independent producers would receive a "fair price" for their work. His strategy: begin modestly and build from there.

In the bars that evening, the consensus was that this was the best "public job application ever made." It had appealed to all interested parties: broadcasters, government, and producers. But it did not deliver to the independents all that it wanted. Debate was intense.

At the end of the festival, it was announced that the Home Secretary would address all these issues at the Royal Television

Society's Cambridge Convention two weeks hence. What Whitelaw had to say brought joy to many an independent heart: the fourth channel should be "supplied by organizations and persons other than the companies contracted to supply programmes on ITV-1." Victory!

When the call went out for a chief executive for the new Channel Four, Jeremy Isaacs was the front-runner. His prescription for the channel:

- To encourage innovation across the whole range of programs;
- To find audiences for the channel and for all its programs;
- To make programs of special appeal to particular audiences;
- To develop the channel's educational potential to the full;
- To provide platforms for the widest possible range of opinions in utterance, discussion, and debate;
- To maintain as flexible a schedule as practicable to enable a quick response to changing needs;
- To make an opening in the channel for criticism of its own output;
- To accord a high priority to the arts;
- If funds allow, to make, or help make, films of feature length for television here, for the cinema abroad.

Two candidates though likely to apply were Charles Denton from ATV and Brian Wenham from BBC. But they did not apply. From the many other candidates, three were chosen for final interview and all were program makers: Isaacs, Paul Bonner, head of BBC Science and Features and John Birt, director of programs at London Weekend Television. I recall talking by phone from

Canada with Jeremy the night before of his interview. He was polishing his shoes. He observed that if he did not get the job, he would join the ranks of independent producers "just like you." He got the job. The chairman urged him to take on Bonner as part of the channel's management, which he did. John Birt, in due course, became director-general of the BBC.

While the launch of Channel Four in 1982 solved a problem for the UK independent sector, it took another government commission for BBC and ITV to fully accept the role of independent producers. Margaret Thatcher wanted to "do something" about the BBC, believing that it should be supported by advertising. She appointed a classic liberal economist, Professor Alan Peacock, to head the enquiry and it was assumed he would do her bidding and privatize the BBC.

While British television thrived on competition, it was nonetheless a public service system in which commercial imperatives should not be the sole determinant of program content. As Michael Darlow records in his book *Independents Struggle*, "in countries which had modelled their broadcasting systems on Britain where … advertising had been introduced into the main public service broadcast systems, such as CBC in Canada and ABC in Australia, the result had been the steady degradation and increasing marginalization of their public service broadcasters." Contrary to expectations, Peacock recommended in 1986 that BBC Television should not be obliged to finance its operations by advertising: this would reduce the range of choice available to viewers. The ITV franchises, on the other hand, were to be put out to competitive tender on a regular basis, a more Thatcherite policy.

The independent producers' lobbying agenda had focused on access to both BBC and ITV. Importantly, Peacock concluded that BBC and ITV must take 40 percent of their programs from independents. In Jeremy Isaacs' words "The British independent filmmaker has been treated very snottily by the BBC and ITV over the years and now we have an absolute triumph of the work." Channel Four was that triumph, and now there were to be quotas for BBC and ITV. Yet another victory!

While it took the Brits a long time to get their way, it represented a true transformation of the UK production sector. Jeremy Isaacs' conclusion is instructive: "To their great credit, 99 percent of independent producers did deliver on time and on budget. Some made poorish programmes, some good, some marvellous. Few made fortunes. All, in a sense, did well; a decade previously no one believed they could do it at all."

In Canada the Broadcast Program Development Fund was our great leap forward, but we never got an equivalent to the UK's Channel Four, which paid full cost for commissions plus 15 percent. Nor did we get a strict requirement that all broadcasters accept a substantial and specific quota of independent production. But, for our efforts, we too did well and built what is now a $12 billion industry from a standing start.

CHAPTER 11

NEXT STAGES

I HAD ALWAYS BEEN AN avid theatre-goer, and one of Primedia's early successes was a TV adaptation of the Edinburgh Festival's hit musical *Billy Bishop Goes to War*, a co-production with BBC Scotland with a tiny acquisition fee supplied by the CBC at the last moment. It won us ACTRA's Nellie award for the best television program of the year. The prize was presented to us by Prime Minister Pierre Elliot Trudeau. The CBC won the eighteen other awards, but were pissed off at losing the big one, which was compounded by the fact that, in my excitement, I forgot to acknowledge their tiny contribution in my acceptance speech.

Another theatrical adaption was John Murrell's *Waiting for the Parade*, directed by Robin Phillips with an all-female cast of Donna Goodhand, Martha Henry, Sheila McCarthy, Carole Shelley, and Susan Wright. Theatre and dance productions were rewarding because the material was already tested with audiences, the performers knew their characters inside out, and the challenge was how to adapt them to the small screen. Sometimes TV could add things that the live experience could not do. Watching a ballet in a theatre, the audience's attention might wander across the stage, whereas on the small screen one could focus attention on specific movements. It was a choreographer's dream.

It was during these first Primedia years that I developed my association with the National Ballet of Canada and with Canada's National Ballet School, where I became a trustee and remain a member of its Honorary Circle. Marcia McClung, granddaughter of Nellie McClung, the suffragette and social activist, was then the communications director for the National Ballet and she called me up asking for a meeting. I invited her to lunch at a restaurant that looked like a gazebo off the lobby of the Royal York Hotel. She had a brief to explore how to broaden the appeal of the company. In our conversation, we discussed ways of televising ballet despite the hostility and prohibitive costs of the various performing unions, the American Federation of Musicians, and in particular, the International Association of Theatrical Stage Employees (IATSE) representing the stagehands. For every dollar a dancer earned from a television performance, a musician would earn double and a stagehand four times what the dancer earned. I had discovered this abomination when dealing with the Royal Ballet in the UK. I was making a documentary about Canadian ballerina Lynn Seymour and wanted to film a *pas de deux* on stage at Covent Garden. I was told I would have to pay the stagehands even though we would not be using any sets. I asked how many stagehands would be required and was told that every stagehand who had been employed at the Royal Opera House that entire season would have to be paid. We rented a studio across town, brought in a dance floor, and recorded our session without benefit of stagehands.

The challenge was to persuade stagehands that television was not the enemy: it was a promotion of live performance, would broaden the audience and make their futures more secure not less. And my assertion proved to be correct. But Marcia and I had to plot together to thwart and then convince IATSE's Jimmy Fuller at the O'Keefe Centre. In time Primedia was able to shoot dance (and opera) without audience using the O'Keefe stage as our studio, assisted by Jimmy's stagehands.

Our first venture, before solving the O'Keefe situation, was to shoot *Newcomers: The Ballet* choreographed by Brian McDonald for the National Ballet of Canada, based on our television series of the same name and using music from the series. We shot it at the Shaw Festival Theatre in Niagara-on-the-Lake. Brian directed the television show. I have always wanted to intimately involve the choreographer or artistic director of the company in the conception and direction of any television adaptation. I have had the pleasure of working with Alexander Grant, Eric Bruhn, Reid Anderson, James Kudelka, Glen Tetley, and many others. For most of my ballet productions, Norman Campbell was the television director.

Together Marcia and I agreed upon a strategy that saw me become the television advisor to the National Ballet (and later to the Canadian Opera Company) producing full-length ballets (and operas) for the CBC and documentaries for the BBC and others, many starring the amazing Karen Kain, who had turned me on to ballet in the first place.

Though Pay TV had been a disaster in Canada, some producers did enjoy success with a major US Pay TV service: Home Box Office (HBO). Unlike a broadcaster, which must find audience and advertisers for each individual program, a subscription service like HBO depends on offering enough attractive programs to prevent audience members from cancelling their subscriptions (known as "churn") rather than trying to achieve high ratings for every program. If you were a boxing fan, you might be content to watch boxing matches alone and not worry about all the other programs. If you got value, you would continue to subscribe. Pay TV needs to please all of its audience but only some of the time. HBO offered movies, but so did other channels; to set itself apart, it needed original programming, and Canada was one place to find it. In fact, HBO owed its rise to prominence partly to Canadian-produced television movies, the first being Robert Cooper's *The Terry Fox Story*.

One of Primedia's productions for HBO was *Countdown to Looking Glass* (later sold to First Choice in Canada). The plot imagined the onset of a Third World War, seen through the eyes of CTN, a fictional cable news network we had invented about the same time Ted Turner was launching the real CNN. The film starred Scott Glenn, Michael Murphy, and Helen Shaver with Patrick Watson as the news anchor and real journalists such as Eric Sevareid and Nancy Dickerson as correspondents. To reflect the realities of the time we shot in three different formats: in the studio on one-inch tape, the fictional correspondents' reports on 16-mm film, and the action of the movie itself in 35 mm. I am not sure if anyone spotted this attempt at verisimilitude, but the film won the ACE Award that year for best cable TV drama in the United States.

Pay TV had a major creative impact. Most TV drama series in North America were written with commercials in mind, so that one had to have cliffhangers to bring the audience back after a commercial. Dramatic writing for network television became formulaic.

Pay TV freed up writers to break out of this straitjacket and to stretch their imaginations in form, content, and subject matter. When HBO commissioned David Chase to create *The Sopranos*, its future was secured.

Another drama experience for me was with the National Film Board of Canada. I joined director Claude Fournier (with whom I had worked on *The New Avengers* and *The Newcomers/Les Arrivants*) and his brilliant production partner Marie-José Raymond in an adaptation of Gabrielle Roy's *Bonheur D'Occasion/The Tin Flute*, with Marilyn Lightstone in the principal role. This NFB experience was more pleasant than previous ones, because we were shooting in Montreal with a top Québécois producer who knew who was good at the NFB and more importantly who to avoid. The project required us to shoot a movie in English and one in French as well as two five-hour mini-series versions for television. In the process, I learned a lot about the need for uncompromising toughness of mind from Marie-José!

A co-production with UK bookseller Dorling Kindersley, *The Amateur Naturalist*, resulted in our best natural history series with Gerry and Lee Durrell in addition to a splendidly illustrated book. The experience inspired Gerry to write, with his own inimitable humour, an account of the production called *How to Shoot an Amateur Naturalist.* The two producers responsible, Primedia's Paula Quigley and DK's Jonathan Harris, fell in love and in due course were married. Paula continued to work for me and later Jonathan joined her in Canada to work for Primedia.

I had always liked to work with women, especially having produced a highly controversial science documentary entitled *Brain Sex* which explored the differences in the brain structure between men and women. The latter tend on average to have a proportionally larger corpus callosum connecting the two sides of the brain, which might theoretically help to explain male focus and female ability to multitask. Hence there are many more male mathematical geniuses (and more male serial killers) in comparison to women, who are much better able than men to connect emotions and communication. If this were indeed true, I felt that my industry would be better served by more female creative writers and producers. At one stage at the height of Primedia, I had twenty employees, of which nineteen were female. Jonathan, my single male employee, he and I had a stormy relationship, which may have been male competitiveness at work. Promotion through the ranks was something I always encouraged, my secretaries developing into fine executive assistants and then story editors, line producers, creative producers, and so on. Primedia was way ahead of the industry curve in offering opportunity to female talent.

Back in Toronto, Dick continued to write screenplays, one of which we filmed at the King Edward Hotel in the newly refurbished Royal Suite (where Richard Burton and Elizabeth Taylor had spent their honeymoon). *Quebec/Canada 1995* was set a dozen years in the future on the eve of Quebec separating from Canada. The prime minister of Canada, the new president of Quebec, and the secretary general of the United Nations were dining together with their wives and of course discussing how this separation had come about. It was a great vehicle for exploring the tensions between two "nations."

However, tension was also growing between my mentor and me. I was building the business around profitable international co-productions, while Dick wanted to write and then produce his own creations, which did not always make a return in the small Canadian marketplace. Rather than destroy our personal friendship, we decided to go our separate ways, and in 1985, I bought out Dick by assuming the debts of Primedia. Dick started his new operation under the shingle Norflicks Productions, which he ran until his death in 2014. Our friendship endured. I am forever grateful to him.

Before we parted, we received a message from Peter Pearson, then-recently appointed as program director of Telefilm Canada. It read: *Following yesterday's meeting, I went away reflecting on what a significant contribution you both have made, together and separately, to this country. Your long and distinguished careers have rightly garnered you much recognition, both within Canada and abroad. You have brought to Canadian screens and television sets some of the best independent production this country has produced. And we are all in your debt for having done so with such integrity, under such arduous circumstances. You have both fought long and hard for the right of an independent sector to exist. You have argued the causes, fought through the cases and defended the interests of everybody, with a remarkable degree of persistence and tenacity.*

If there was to be a eulogy on our partnership, who could ask for more?

CHAPTER 12

ON MY OWN (1985–1993)

IN 1985 I WAS forty years old and on my own with a company to build back. My first call was to our British distributor Richard Price in London to tell him that Dick and I had separated. Richard was a true pioneer in the international distribution business, attending the first MIP-TV in Lyon before it moved to Cannes and developed into the world's largest television market. At that first market Richard hand-carried a 16-mm projector and reels of film to display his wares. During the Torstar days he had persuaded Dick and me that we needed him to represent our programming internationally. On reflection, one of our early errors was that Dick and I did not take aftersales seriously enough, always wanting to move on as creators to the next project. Some of our competitors set up their own distribution ventures and it helped them prosper. We did not. But for us the link to Richard Price was manifestly a good move.

Richard's company Richard Price Television Associates (RPTA) had a production arm called Primetime, led by an impressive managing director David Elstein, a prodigiously talented producer (nicknamed "two-brains Elstein") who went on to become director of programming at Thames Television and BSkyB before being appointed as chief executive of Channel Five. One of Primetime's greatest achievements was an adaptation of the National Theatre production of *The Life and Adventures of Nicholas Nickleby* for Channel Four, produced by Colin Callender, who ended up as president of HBO Films. Richard hired good people and his love of the stage saw him continue producing with the Royal National Theatre's Trevor Nunn such musicals as *Oklahoma!* and *Porgy and Bess*. He was an early investor in *The King's Speech*, and I will tell later of his involvement in another theatrical megahit.

After Dick and I split up, my call to RP elicited this response: "Would you like an equity investor? And will you change your company name to Primetime?" RP was always direct and to the point. I said yes to the former as I needed funds to pay down the debt I had taken on (RPTA became a minority shareholder) and I said would have to think about the latter. I felt it important to preserve a separate identity, so I eventually declined the name change, but I redesigned our logo and letterhead to show that Primedia was clearly part of the Primetime family. By then RPTA had moved from Albermarle Street to new premises in Seymour Mews, which became my second office. I was specializing in co-productions, particularly with the British, and was in London at least one week in every six. Thus, if any British producer was looking for co-production financing, I made sure Primedia was at the top of their mind when it came to Canada.

At this point, Richard's previous partner, Arthur Marmor was gone and the new partner was a former merchant banker Richard

Leworthy, some three years younger than me. While some called them Big Richard (Price) and Little Richard (Leworthy), most referred to them as RP and RL. RL became a close personal friend and helped me through both good times and bad.

RL had clearly been a success in his previous career, with all the trappings of a prosperous businessman: a house in West London, a copious wine cellar, a yacht on the Hamble, a power boat in La Napoule near his summer home on the main square of Valbonne, the richest village in France. RL's club was Boodle's, he went on shooting parties, and he drove a Ferrari, then a Bentley. Richard wore all this effortlessly and never flaunted his good fortune. Instead, he shared it. He let me stay with him and his wife Judy in his house in Shepherd's Bush, where their son Felix walked in on me while I was taking a bath, jumped in with his rubber ducky, and observed, "You are very fat!" He spoke the truth. On a couple of occasions when times were tight, I took my family (five of us) to the South of France for the March break. Our flights were paid for with Aeroplan points, and RL loaned us his Valbonne home and a car he kept in France.

When RL decided to move up in the world and purchased a home in Hammersmith Grove, I helped him move, the two of us literally carrying his many wine racks by hand from one home to the next. When his children, Felix and Sam, were grown, Richard finally came to rest with a home in Chiswick. I had a key to each house in turn, and was privileged to have the Leworthys as my second family and their homes as my second homes. Sadly, Richard died from Motor Neurone Disease (ALS) just as the COVID pandemic struck. My last flight before lockdown was to see Richard prior to his death. He was a brilliant mind, a genuinely good man, and a great friend. I truly miss him.

RP was also generous. I would often stay late at the RPTA office, where RP let me use their phone lines to keep in touch with Toronto, which was generally five hours behind London. I was not the only producer to win permission to use RP's phones. Judy Clayton was developing a musical, and RP had made a small investment in the project. Judy's calls were primarily to a band in Sweden. Her idea was to do a stage play based on the band's music. The band she was talking to was ABBA and the musical became *Mamma Mia*. What a great investment by RP.

Primedia's first major drama production during this period was *Frontier* (originally titled *Les Aventuriers de la Baie d'Hudson*), a six-hour mini-series co-produced with Telecip in France and HTV in the UK. Eventually, there were eighteen partners in nine countries, including nine partners in Canada whom I had to keep in line. The production's T-shirt had the first nine partners on the front followed by the word "over" and then the other partners on the back. It was exhausting keeping track of them all.

One of the partners was Telefilm Canada, run by Peter Pearson, my mentor from the *Document* days. Though he had fully acknowledged that his new Broadcast Program Development Fund was the product of my "third envelope" concept, he was not content to let broadcasters rule exclusively on editorial content. Even though I had all my financing in place, Peter started to raise questions about the *Frontier* scripts, which caused Global to have some second thoughts even though they had already committed to the production. I had to drive into Toronto from a vacation cottage for an emergency meeting to plead with Paul Morton, then running Global. Much to my relief, he agreed to honour the commitment that his employees had made. I sometimes feel that being an independent producer demands four skills all beginning the letter

"B": bravado, bullshit, blackmail, and begging. *Frontier* was a nightmare production that required the last quality in full measure.

Frontier began with a French company, Telecip, whose producers Jacques Dercourt (who became a wonderful friend) and Roland Gritti had developed it with two French writers. It was instructive to see how Gritti behaved in writers' meetings, treating them as if they were schoolboys who had produced inferior homework. After each meeting with much scolding and firm instruction by Gritti, I took the writers away to recover and we engaged in much friendlier discussions on how to produce improved scripts that would satisfy Gritti and our UK partner, HTV. I managed all this in French, as our writers did not speak English. When each draft script was ready, it was translated and then polished. However, despite assurances that our French leading actor was fluent in English, he wasn't. Our two other leads were Italian and German, both with adequate English, and the director was Russian. Despite his indecision during pre-production, I was assured that all would proceed smoothly once we were in production.

We started filming in the newly completed heritage reconstruction in Louisbourg in Cape Breton. The director told me his first shot would be on a tripod pointing in one direction. When I got to set on day one, he was laying track and pointing in the opposite direction. Our English line producer was not impressed and hounded the director unmercifully. We discovered that the director did not know how to manage the numerous costumed extras we had engaged to show a bustling community: for some reason they were always behind his camera! At one stage I called a summit meeting with my French and British partners to argue for a change in the director. I was out-voted: one of the risks of co-production.

When the shoot moved to France, I saw that the crew's notion of tracking shots meant strapping a tripod on a wooden dolly as opposed to Canada's thoroughly professional equipment. Then our director had a heart attack and died; his widow would not allow the line producer to attend the funeral, claiming that stress had caused her husband's demise. A replacement French director was engaged for the remaining French shoot and then for the British shoot. He was more than competent. I hired a Canadian director for the second Canadian shoot, and we managed to complete the series and had decent reviews. We ultimately lost money on the project, but the cash flow during production kept us alive as I built back the company. *Frontier* is the one production I have never had the courage to screen again (too much pain), although my son Andrew took a look at it when he was going to be filming at Louisbourg for *Captain Cook*, and he said the series was actually quite good.

One of the positive outcomes of working with Telecip and HTV was the creation of a "co-production club" called Vision, a word that worked both in English and French. We invited a German company TV60, run by Claus Hardt, and Alessandro Fracassi's Italian company Racing Pictures, to join us. We agreed to meet three times a year to share and compare potential projects: the first two meetings took place in Cannes in April and October, and for our third meeting, one of the partners would host a splendid gathering in the summer on home territory. It was a chance for each of the European partners to show off their country's best cuisine. The French led off with a sumptuous dinner in Paris hosted by Roland Gritti, whose family was descended from Doge Andrea Gritti, who, in 1525, acquired the fourteenth century Gritti Palace in Venice. Next up was Patrick Dromgoole, the managing director and then chairman of HTV, who rented the caves in Bristol where John Harvey and Sons, the wine merchants who created Harvey's Bristol Cream, imported their product. A splendid feast was served. Alessandro Fracassi's family home was used as the Japanese Embassy during the Second World War. We had an impeccable outdoor luncheon in a gazebo in the luxurious gardens. When my turn came, I used the Banff Television Festival, set in the Rocky Mountains, as the venue. While Vision was a wonderful supper club, we never co-produced a project that included all five partners. But we did co-produce a number of two-way and three-way ventures that benefited each participating partner.

Co-production was my primary means of doing business. Its detractors dismissed co-production as a synonym for creative compromise, but I saw it another way. With the fragmenting of television audiences, the only strategy to sustain reasonable budgets was through collaboration. Canadians have become experts in co-production. We had to be, given our proximity to the United States. Communications networks rapidly lead to trade in culture, and trade in culture raises fears for national sovereignty. As Canada's great communications guru Harold Innis observed, Canada had been skilled in the business of trading from its earliest days, but we were less skilled in protecting the content of that trade. We exported our talent to Hollywood and imported American programming. Thus, for me, co-production with other countries was a key tool in industry-building.

At conferences, I could always get a laugh describing Canada as itself a co-production, one in which we could have enjoyed American technology, British government, and French culture, the best of all possible worlds. Instead, the Fathers of Confederation missed the boat and we ended up with British technology, French government, and American culture. The point I was making was that America had produced the most energetic and expansionist culture the world has ever known: Coca Cola, Elvis Presley, McDonald's, Disneyland, *Star Wars,* and on and on. But rather than get depressed, we should accept that the appeal of American entertainment resides in its authenticity as an expression of its culture. The question is how to compete and authentically preserve our own culture. For me, once again, the answer lay ironically in co-production.

To succeed, we needed confidence in our talent, a determination to create popular programming, matched by supportive governmental incentives and tax breaks. Canada led the world in innovative subsidies and tax credits. This enabled us to play at the top table with partners in the UK and Europe, and then further afield. Whether we were telling our own stories like *Heaven on Earth* or *Glory Enough for All,* or drawing from our own literature as with Kevin Sullivan's *Anne of Green Gables,* Canadians were doing this authentically but utilizing foreign funding as well as our own: in the first two examples, with substantial British funding, and in the last case, German partners. We became skilled at marrying the tastes of different audiences and matching American production values. Among the incentives and innovative polices were federal and provincial agencies which invested, then federal and provincial tax credit regimes, co-production treaties and twinning, as well as co-ventures of all shapes and sizes. Canada benefited, as did other partner countries, and the fruits of these collaborations were sold into the US market. It was win-win-win.

The creation of Telefilm Canada had helped independent producers and had stirred the pot at the CBC, whose producers for the first time felt genuinely challenged. In March 1987, I was one of a group of independent producers invited by CBC vice president Denis Harvey to speak at a CBC Retreat at the Deerhurst Inn on the edge of Algonquin Park. I argued for protection of the CBC's distinctiveness and for its publisher function, but stated that as far as I could see the government would not give the CBC more money, at least not until the Corporation had changed. I said I agreed with a then-recent article by Robert Fulford, who said that the key was not the money available to the CBC, but "allocation of resources" within the CBC. I pursued a similar theme: redistribute resources within the Corporation. Don't try to be all things to all people. Make some hard choices. Use the independents with Telefilm Canada funding for dramatic storytelling.

My prescription for the CBC's English Services Division was as follows

1. Be Canadian: But not narrow. All the world is our stage, but the perspective must be Canadian and not imitative.
2. Be Popular: And popularity should be defined not by ratings, but by reach. It must provide a popular alternative to American television.
3. Be Distinctive: The CBC can no longer duplicate what the private sector can do.
4. Be Talent-Led: Forge close relationships with talent in all its forms including major arts organizations. They are your natural allies, as are independent producers, who are not your competitors but your partners.
5. Be National: Audiences don't want regional drama if that means inferior drama. The CBC's drama should reflect every part of the country, but don't try to build film industries or program departments in every province. Look at

the United States. They have Hollywood and New York, because that is where the experienced creators and crews are concentrated. This may offend a Canadian sense of fairness, but this is not about being fair, it is about being good.

6. Be International: This is not in conflict with its being Canadian or national. Why not showcase the best in the world rather than just American programming?
7. Be Commercial-Free: A difficult recommendation in times of restraint, but a real signal that change is on the way.

I ended by quoting my godfather Leonard Brockington, the first chairman of the CBC, who pointed out in a speech in 1939 that "the importance of avoiding duplication of facilities and concentrating all available sources of revenue … on the production of Canadian programs. The system it conceived might be described as 'public ownership of stations, competition in programs." He added: "that advertising and the profit motive should not be the foundations on which this new medium of mass communication should be built."

Mine was a provocative speech and I am told that it encouraged intense and wide-ranging debate for the balance of the retreat. We were not permitted to stay to hear what was said, but were returned to Toronto by the same limousine that had brought us, in the midst of a huge snowstorm.

CHAPTER 13

THE PROVINCES STEP UP/ THE SPECIALTIES STEP IN

JUST A FEW MONTHS earlier in 1986, provincial jurisdictions became involved in film and television funding, which certainly enhanced Canada's bargaining power in the international production game. Primedia was the first applicant to the newly formed Ontario Film Development Corporation (OFDC) with *Heaven on Earth*, the Margaret Atwood film we had been trying to make for so long. This led to an awkward meeting with Bernard Ostry, then a deputy minister in the Ontario Government. Bernie had been my Dad's research assistant on his critical biography *The Age of Mackenzie King*. My father wrote every word of the book, but generously offered Bernie co-author credit, whereupon Bernie tried to persuade the publisher to put his name first. The co-authors fought bitterly and never spoke to each other again. I became the go-between relaying Bernie's messages to Dad and his responses. On this occasion, Bernie had got wind of my father's forthcoming autobiography *Reading from Left to Right*, which included a devastating chapter on his dealings with Ostry. Bernie invited me to lunch at Il Posto, a fancy Italian restaurant in Yorkville, where he reflected on how unfortunate the falling out had been between Dad and him, and that it was a pity Dad had never been invited to be a visiting professor at the University of Toronto, which is something he could arrange. Could I please pass on his message? Going further, Bernie shared that the OFDC would soon be in business and that I would be an early beneficiary. I knew that I would, on my own merit and not as a favour. My father did not take up Bernie's largesse and the offending chapter was passed by the libel lawyers and is in the book unchanged.

As a new bureaucracy, the OFDC wanted the independent producers to complete and photocopy a huge number of forms to spare their own staff spending all their time at the photocopier. As I recall, OFDC asked for everything to be delivered in quadruplicate: four copies of the screenplay, four copies of the full production budget, and so on. It took several banker's boxers to hold all the stuff. Wayne Clarkson, the new executive director, took one look at our application, which we delivered in person, and observed: "Oh dear! We have a major problem. We don't have nearly enough storage space for all the applications that are going to come in." And it wasn't too long before they moved from their small fashionable coach house accommodations to expanded offices in a high-rise office block with sufficient storage space.

Around that time, I was interviewed by Granada Television for a history of television they were producing. After they were finished with me, I asked if I could put a question to them. It was this: "What is distinctive about Canadian television?" Quick as a flash, the producer answered: "The Canadian television industry produces more paper than any other." Our bureaucratic tendencies were exposed for all to see!

The reason for all the paperwork was that rather than a single broadcaster commissioning and paying full price for a production (as was the case with Channel Four in the UK), we Canadian independents usually required multiple sources to finance our films. Even on an international co-production, we might need a couple of Canadian broadcasters, federal and provincial tax credits, Telefilm Canada and a provincial fund, plus other funds or sponsors just to raise the Canadian share. Each institution had different rules which had to be harmonized, all institutions required application forms and accompanying documentation, and all required contracts: a feast for the legal profession. No wonder I often felt that business affairs trumped creative concerns.

It was a relief to finally realize *Heaven on Earth*, which I optioned from Peter Pearson when he was an independent producer. After thirteen years of effort and a creative breakthrough that had improved the script, I was ready. When the film was still part of my dealings with Yorkshire Television. David Cunliffe thought the script might benefit from some work with a script editor, something I had never used up until that point. Margaret Atwood was unable to attend the meeting due to a last-minute scheduling conflict, but I decided to proceed and met with the script editor in London. She had been through the screenplay meticulously and had in front of her a series of coloured index cards. Each card summarized a scene from the script and the colours indicated whether it was a necessary scene or not, which scenes needed some re-writing or not, scenes that were missing, and so forth.

We spent the day debating her advice, revising where necessary, and finally agreeing what would make the film better.

I returned to Toronto with a pack of coloured cards and scheduled a meeting with Peggy Atwood at her home, then on Sullivan Street. It took me about forty-five minutes to explain what we had worked on in London. Peggy absorbed it, made a few suggestions, and then concluded, "I've got it." About a week later, the screenplay came back and it worked like a dream. Rewriting does not always go so smoothly.

BBC Wales Head of Drama John Hefin loved the revised screenplay and agreed to make the film, but to make the financing work, we needed to twin it with another project. Fortuitously, Terry Ryan, a Canadian expat living in London, had approached me with a script called *Going Home* that needed to be shot in Wales.

Terry's script was about a celebrated mutiny of Canadian soldiers in the Camp Kinmell repatriation camp after the First World War. It was a good script with a great role for the ringleader of the mutiny. We cast Nicholas Campbell (later to achieve celebrity as the coroner in *Da Vinci's Inquest*) as our lead for *Going Home.* Nick always called it his finest screen performance. Also in the cast were two young Canadian actors in their first major roles: Milan Cheylov and Albert Schultz. I was called off set during *Going Home* to confront charges that Schultz was a murderer. It turned out there was a murderer of the same name on the loose and a British tabloid gave front page coverage to their unresearched story: "BBC hires murderer for TV movie!" When it was demonstrated that they had fingered the wrong man, the apology was buried in the inside pages. What irresponsibility!

Going Home and *Heaven on Earth* were both stories of displacement and perfect for twinning.

Heaven on Earth was shot mainly in Canada with Welsh actors playing the orphans, although one of our Canadian cast members was Sarah Polley, later the star of *Road to Avonlea* and now a terrific writer and film director. *Going Home* was shot in Wales with a mainly Canadian cast playing soldiers. Both directors, Allan Kroeker on the former and Terry Ryan on the latter, were Canadian. And the expenses were fairly evenly spread between the two countries, so we achieved Canadian Content status. These were the first Canadian films screened on BBC's prestigious *Screen Two* and were extremely well received by audiences both on the BBC and on the CBC in Canada. *Heaven on Earth* was the first Canadian production on PBS *Masterpiece Theatre*. Allan Kroeker and I were awarded the Quebec-Alberta prize.

One anecdote to relate from the production of *Heaven on Earth*: Allan Kroeker had a tradition of casting his producer (in this case me) in a small role in all his films. He asked me to play the Captain on the ship bringing the orphans to Canada. I declined. He asked me why. I said that all his previous producers had a line or two of dialogue whereas the Captain had no lines and was in effect just an extra. Next morning a pink page (script revision) arrived on my desk. The Captain now had a line! I agreed to participate. With a speaking part, I now had to be paid as an actor, so I donated this extra money to the production's wrap party. I did enjoy being fitted for a naval uniform in which I looked impressive. In the final version of the film, my line ended up on the cutting room floor. But I have a photo of myself and my two older children, Andrew and Katharine, who performed as extras. Our casting director saw them come into the office as we were going on to a family event after work. She immediately said, "those look like orphans" (thank you very much!) and offered them work. My youngest son

Mark went on to be an actor, but he was the one who declined to participate, as he thought it would be boring. But Andrew and Katharine liked the money they earned.

During this time, I was helping to program the conference portion of the Banff Television Festival. One year I thought we should ask producers to talk about a success and a failure. Failures are usually more instructive, but producer egos are such that you have to offer the good if you want them to reveal the bad. As I feared, most people's successes were genuine successes while their "failures" were most often disguised successes or small failures. To set an example I thought I should talk about *Heaven on Earth* and *Grey Owl*, on both of which I laboured for a dozen or more years: one got made, the other did not. It is a cruel fact that in this business, many of your "babies" die. I persevered with *Grey Owl* with a multitude of potential UK partners, with multiple versions of the script at differing lengths, coming close on various occasions. Part of the problem was expense: we would have to film across at least two seasons and in two countries. I analyzed my failure and hoped it was of some value to my fellow producers.

A couple of months later I received a message from Richard Attenborough, whose movie *Gandhi* I much admired. He asked me to come to his Richmond home on the outskirts of London next time I was in town. As I entered through the gates outside his imposing house, I saw that it was called Beaver Lodge. The reason he wanted to see me was a plan to shoot a film on Grey Owl. Richard and his brother David had both seen the real Grey Owl perform in Oxford when they were children. Dickie (as he was called) had been acquiring rights to various books by and about Grey Owl and a key volume was *Wilderness Man* to which I held the rights. Thinking that there might be a co-production in this, I was most cooperative and made a generous deal, promising him our various drafts of the screenplay, location survey notes and pictures, and indeed anything that might help get the project produced. It was a friendly meeting, but once rights had been acquired, it quickly became evident that Dickie wanted to do this on his own. It took him quite some time to get it financed and regrettably a rather insipid movie resulted with Pierce Brosnan in the lead. I thought my Banff "failure" presentation might have converted itself into a success, but, as it turned out for me *Grey Owl* was still a failure.

I did, however, get to meet Dickie's brother David when we presented him the Award of Excellence at Banff many years later. Jenny and I had dinner with him alone one night at the Banff Springs Hotel, giving her the chance to meet another of her childhood heroes, the other being Gerry Durrell, for whom she worked in setting up his Canadian fundraising arm Wildlife Preservation Trust Canada, which still continues the quest to save endangered species from extinction.

The next important report on Canadian media was the Caplan-Sauvageau report, commissioned by Marcel Masse and the Conservatives in 1986. Its conclusions were not a surprise. They declared that despite technological advances, the struggle continued unabated to find a truly Canadian voice in the media. The reasons cited were the familiar refrain: small market, two languages, and the tension between public and private interests. The report called for a new Broadcasting Act, which Flora Macdonald eventually delivered in 1991.

Meanwhile, changes were coming faster in the cable business than in broadcast television and throughout this whole period my lobbying went on. Over the years, the funding formulas had begun to require participation from everyone in Canadian broadcasting, and cable operators were no exception. Cable providers had grown their businesses in part by providing better signals for American broadcasters, which only increased competition for Canadian producers. Cable operators were now required to allocate percentages of revenue to Canadian Content production.

In 1993 Phil Lind of Rogers was appointed by the Canadian Cable Television Association to come up with an industry-wide Cable Fund. He and I met at an Italian restaurant in Toronto's theatre district to discuss how this should work. He proposed to model the Cable Fund on the Broadcast Fund of Telefilm Canada. Thus, cable industry funding would be treated as an equity investment. I pointed out that if broadcasters and Telefilm and the Cable Fund (and subsequently the Provincial Funds) all took equity, there would be nothing left as an upside for independent producers from which to develop new ideas or build sustainable businesses. Even with Telefilm Canada, a provincial agency, a broadcaster and the Cable Fund putting up their share, producers needed to find additional funding or defer their fees, leaving foreign sales as the only potential revenue. If all the financiers were taking their share of equity, there would never be any real upside for the producers.

Phil was a good man and always protected the interests of Rogers and the cable industry, but he also had a strong sense of community. Throughout his time with Rogers, he and Ted Rogers had made sure there was a viable future for independent producers. This was demonstrated through the Rogers Telefund and other funds they created. What Phil and I worked out for this new industry fund was memorialized on a paper napkin: a proportion of the Cable Fund contribution would be a grant (a supplement to the low licence fees we received from Canadian broadcasters), to be called the Licence Fee Program (LFP), and a proportion would be treated as an equity investment, called the Equity Investment Program (EIP).

In the fullness of time, the government saw the benefits of public-private partnerships, and it was proposed that the Broadcast Fund of Telefilm Canada and the Cable Fund be merged as the Canadian Television and Cable Production Fund (CTCPF). At a hastily arranged 1996 industry gathering to explain this new partnership, I handed over to Phil the paper napkin on which we had structured the Cable Fund, which would be continued in the CTCPF. The organization was renamed the Canada Media Fund in 2010 and is now the largest supporter of the arts in Canada. In 2021–2022 CMF invested over $360 million in independent production.

The growth of cable in the mid-1980s was undermining the dominance of the broadcasters and the industry was embracing the chance to develop specialties. We can see this evolution through the example of Discovery Inc., a group of lifestyle channels and brands in an area one could call specialist factual programming, including Discovery Channel, Animal Planet, Science Channel, and TLC. In the 1990s as it grew, it developed sub-brands such as Discovery Kids, Discovery Health, and the like; and in the new century it bought Scripps Network and added channels such as the Food Network, HGTV, and the Travel Channel. In 2021, AT&T announced its proposal to merge its media subsidiary Warner Media with Discovery, Inc.

Back in the 1980s, Discovery's major competitor was Arts & Entertainment Networks, a merger of ABC/Hearst's ARTS channel and RCA's Entertainment Channel, led by Nickolas Davatzes. From its origins in the fine arts, documentary, drama, and educational programming, it morphed into a platform for reality programming, docusoaps, true crime and similar non-fiction material. In the mid-1990s its pay television service The History Channel, a joint venture between Hearst and Disney, was launched to great acclaim. THC's subsidiary brand Biography was another success.

Discovery expanded worldwide, but its Canadian offshoot is an exception being a joint venture between Bell and ESPN. Discovery Canada has autonomy from its US parent, the only national Discovery franchise that enjoys such a position. A&E also developed globally, but, though available in Canada, it did not have a comparable domestic presence to Discovery Canada. Its History Channel was subject to legal squabbling with History Television Canada, an Alliance Atlantis channel, now owned by Corus.

In both cases, these specialty groups initially represented real opportunity for Canadian independent producers including Primedia, and we took full advantage. But over time their respective journeys moved them further and further away from our strengths and experience. Many Canadian companies benefited. But once they started making programs such as *Ice Road Truckers* or *Pawn Stars*, Primedia was left out. We preferred to make shows about real history.

CHAPTER 14

ARTS AND COMEDIA

PERFORMING ARTS WERE TO become a Primedia specialty, including dance, opera, music, theatre, and visual arts, and for a while we became the largest independent arts producer in the country. We were doing the kind of programming the public broadcaster should have done, but rarely did apart from an occasional Stratford Festival production. The CBC argued costs, but such productions were in fact much cheaper to produce than a TV movie. Or they argued there was no audience for the arts, but much of our arts programming pulled high ratings. But money and audience aside, shouldn't our public broadcaster be letting all regions of the country have access to performances that they would never have a chance to experience. How best can our national companies tour the nation? Or how can one region share in what is happening in another province? On the small screen, of course. Touring the National Ballet of Canada was so expensive that it could not be done annually, nor to more than a few large cities. There are ballet fans in every small community in Canada. But the CBC did not see or embrace the opportunity and left it to us.

I was visited one day by three students to ask advice on their first film. The students were Niv Fichman, Larry Weinstein, and Barbara Willis Sweete who became Rhombus Media, undoubtedly the best arts producers in Canada, whose work won accolades all over the world. I saw just how good they were. Their first film was appropriately titled *Opus 1, Number 1*. It was about Niv's brother, Yuval, then developing his career as a concert pianist. In time Rhombus took over Primedia's pre-eminent position, and deservedly. Niv continues to be one of Canada's finest feature film producers; Larry is still a superb director of arts documentaries; and Barbara is much in demand as a result of her work directing many of the opera productions on *Live from the Met.* The brilliant Sheena Macdonald joined the troika as head of distribution. She and I often found ourselves attending the same festivals around the world and one of our acts at cocktail receptions was for us to "work the crowd" together, with me pitching Rhombus and her pitching Banff!

Our relationship with the National Ballet of Canada was burgeoning, as was the dance company itself. With the BBC we produced a performance documentary called *Bold Steps* which reflected the ambition of the company. The director wanted an in-depth look at what was shaping up to be one of the top ballet ensembles in the world, and did a version of the final Act One *pas de deux* in *Swan Lake* with four successive ballerinas and partners segueing through the piece. I don't think the dancers were enamoured with the idea, each wanted the starring role exclusively for themselves, but the device did make the point of how much depth the company had. The film went on to win the top prize in Padua.

We shot a full-length version of *Onegin* choreographed by Erik Bruhn, who chose a very young dancer, Sabina Allemann, to play the ingenue lead opposite Frank Augustyn in the title role. It was a spectacular success, as was our next full-length ballet, *The Merry Widow* starring the wondrous Karen Kain. I was getting used to the seemingly endless negotiations about television rights. Our choices of repertoire became bolder with the pairing of two Glen Tetley ballets, *Alice* and *La Ronde.* They showed off Karen at her best. This culminated in my second bio-doc *Karen Kain: Prima Ballerina,* for which we brought in her favourite partners for a selection of her finest *pas de deux.*

Funding such films was always a stretch and with German arts impresario Reiner Moritz, I worked out a twinning package in which we each contributed three hours: we supplied the two Tetley ballets plus *Prima Ballerina*, while Reiner brought the two-hour English National Ballet's *Swan Lake* starring Winnipegger Evelyn Hart and a documentary yet to be determined. It was a complex package, but I finally got the CBC on board with the news that the documentary would be on Bill Forsyth. This meant all six hours had strong Canadian connections, as the Scottish film director Bill Forsyth (*Local Hero*) was coming to Canada to shoot his next film *Housekeeping.* For Hugh Gauntlett, Head of Music and Arts at the CBC, this completed the package brilliantly. All six hours had strong Canadian connections.

From time to time, I asked Reiner how things were progressing with Forsyth, and he stalled and stalled. Eventually, he called me to say that Bill was at last starting rehearsals in Paris. "What in the hell is he doing there?" I responded. "He is due to start filming in Vancouver." "What are you talking about?" retorted Reiner. I was talking about Bill Forsyth, the Scottish filmmaker and Reiner was talking about William Forsythe, the American choreographer. I spent a troubled night knowing I would have to break the news to Hugh Gauntlett in the morning. I guess the gods were with me. When I opened my *Globe and Mail* in the morning, I saw the announcement: "National Ballet of Canada commissions new work from William Forsythe." I opened my meeting with Hugh with the words "I have good news and bad news ..." Luckily for me, Hugh saw the humour in the situation: he had commissioned a film from me that did not exist, but now we had a logical sixth hour in the package.

The postscript to this story is that the Forsythe film was not very good, but I was forgiven as the other five hours were magnificent. Years later, I told the story to then Governor General Adrienne Clarkson. She observed that she had always wondered where the Forsythe film came from, as she had edited it and re-edited it shorter and shorter to at least make it viewable for her audience on *Adrienne Clarkson Presents*.

Another ballet I produced during this period was from the Royal Winnipeg Ballet. It was *The Big Top*, choreographed by Jacques Lemay to the music of Victor Davies. From 1983 to 1988, I served on the board of directors of the Desrosiers Dance Theatre while also doing the same for the National Ballet School. Ballet was becoming more and more a part of my life.

It was on account of what I was doing for the National Ballet of Canada that I was invited to lunch with Lotfi Mansouri, the Iranian-born second general director of the Canadian Opera Company. He asked me to become the television advisor to the company and during my tenure we produced *Tosca* and *La Bohème*, and most successfully *The Makropulos Case*. We were up against major productions elsewhere in the world for the former two, but the third was at the time the only recorded production of the work. We also made a film with BBC Wales on Brian McMaster, the opera executive who moved from the Vancouver Opera to manage the Welsh National Opera in Cardiff.

Given what we had accomplished with *Billy Bishop Goes to War* and *Waiting for the Parade*, I launched an initiative to bring Canadian plays to Canadian audiences from coast to coast. I felt that some of the best writing and best stories in the country were being developed by local theatre companies, and wanted people in Vancouver to see what had been developed in Halifax and vice-versa. I managed to put together an extraordinary collection of local private broadcasters from all regions of Canada. With help from Marcia McClung, we persuaded Confederation Life to sponsor *Stage on Screen*, eight full-length productions from Canadian playwrights. At that time private broadcasters were being encouraged by the CRTC to fund drama and received a 50 percent CanCon bonus for doing so. Each broadcaster received sixteen hours of programming which, with the bonus, became twenty-four hours: with three telecasts they had seventy-two hours of Canadian content drama. All of this in return for financing their own local two-hour production. This meant they were paying about $2,000 per hour for the entire package, less than they were paying for their imported American entertainment, and it made them look very good indeed to the CTRC.

Martha Henry introduced each play from the National Arts Centre. The series included a wide range of plays and production techniques. For example, *Letter from Wingfield Farm* by Dan Needles, whose protagonist quits his job as a Toronto stockbroker to head for a hobby farm in rural Ontario, was a one-man *tour de force* for Rod Beattie. Whereas we had shot *Billy Bishop* in such a way that the star could do things that were impossible onstage, such as having a chroma-key conversation with himself in different costumes, Rod did not want any such artifice, so what we shot was video capture of a live event, or what the French call "captation." The plays dealt with issues that were and remain important, such as Wendy Lill's *Sisters*, a tough, uncompromising look at a convent-run First Nations residential school, from the Prairie Theatre Exchange in Winnipeg. We included such classics as John Murrell's *Farther West* and *Legacy/La Maison Suspendue* by Michel Tremblay. I was proud to have pulled this off, but, despite its success, failed to finance a second season.

My interests were in the performing arts, but Primedia did occasionally venture into the visual arts. I am still very moved by Eric Till's *The Sweetest Spring*, a film we made about war artist Alex Colville returning to scenes in Holland, where he painted many of his most famous works.

In the classical music field, I embarked on a journey to record the five Beethoven piano concertos with five different Canadian soloists and five regional orchestras from across Canada, but only managed André Laplante performing the Emperor concerto with the Vancouver Symphony. Money was getting tighter through the 1980s and arts productions became more and more tricky to finance.

During this period, I convinced myself that I could sell anything, or at least I could always dream up a scenario to finance a production. Hubris maybe, but part of a producer's talent is to find innovative ways to make things happen, and I could often envisage strange combinations of partners to provide financing, especially since my work had gained me access to so many industry decision-makers in Canada and around the world. Sometimes knowing the right people would help me be in the right place at the right time to make a deal.

One such example was hearing about a concept from two Scottish producers, Douglas Eadie and Mike Alexander. Called *The TransAtlantic Sessions*, it proposed to feature a house band led by two extraordinary fiddle players, Scotland's Aly Bain and America's Jay Unger, to which the series would add major folk, rock, and traditional artists from the Celtic World and North America. They would explore their musical roots and would combine to make beautiful sounds together. The house band we created to work with Aly and Jay included Jerry Douglas, an amazing dobro player, and the fantastic acoustic guitarist Russ Bahrenberg. We engaged many exceptional artists including Emmy-Lou Harris and the McGarrigle Sisters. (Kate brought along her then teenage son, Rufus Wainwright, who joined in.) We lodged cast, crew, and band in the Montgreenan Mansion House Hotel in Ayrshire during golf's off-season. It became a very special world. At one point we had about twenty fiddlers playing together!

To get the financing, I managed to bring Global to the table for a one-hour special, but that was all it could be persuaded to commission, and we were able to get BBC Scotland to help finance the full seven half-hour series. Each morning some of the revolving roster of guests got together for breakfast and discussed repertoire, planning to sing harmony on each other's selections. They would share their ideas with Aly and Jay, who in turn would sit down with the house band. Arrangements were discussed and mid-morning we would start shooting: all on film, not video, in an intimate setting, all in close-up. It truly captured the pure joy of music-making. The artists loved it. Anna McGarrigle observed that this was "a musician's idea of paradise."

Another fortuitous coming-together was with American Anglophile Donald L. Taffner, to whom I had been introduced some years earlier. Don was an independent distributor and producer of television programming and live theatre attractions, who handled the distribution of Thames Television, one of the two franchises sharing the lucrative ITV market in London. Don's initial claim to fame was bringing *The Benny Hill Show* to the United States, and in the 1970s he negotiated a deal with Thames Television under which Taffner's company would produce an American version of ITV's *Man about the House*, which became ABC's mega hit *Three's Company* starring John Ritter and Suzanne Somers. Later he negotiated a similar deal to adapt Thames' *Keep It in the Family* as ABC's *Too Close for Comfort*.

When I encountered Don, he had been developing a franchise for horseracing fans based on the novels of Dick Francis, and in 1987 we entered into a new joint venture, called Comedia, to produce three *Dick Francis Mysteries* starring Ian McShane. Don had other ideas for comedy and drama projects that never got off the ground, but something else did.

Don was a producer of game show formats and had hired a producer, Mark Maxwell-Smith, to develop formats for him out of Los Angeles. In 1988 the CBC was looking for afternoon game show formats, and picked up Comedia's pilot for *Talkabout*, hosted by Wayne Cox. Now I would receive an education in the mysteries of game show production. Our deal was to use the CBC Studios in Vancouver, so Comedia rented office space downtown, not too far from the studio. We hired the experienced variety director Michael Watt and with Mark they trained a team of young filmmakers and aspiring students, keen to get into television. Mark knew everything there was to know about game shows: he could talk of little else.

Talkabout had two teams of two persons (friends, couples, whatever) competing against each other. One team was placed in seclusion as the two members of the other team tried under intense time pressure to identify as many words as they could associated with the subject we had given them to "talk about." Each time one of our words was identified, there was an audio cue to affirm they had found it. After the allotted time, the other team were shown the words the first team had failed to mention. If the second team could identify the subject, they stole the points the first team had earned. The entertainment was in the bizarre associations that came into the minds of our competitors as they desperately tried to beat the clock.

As Mark explained to me, the formula for a successful game show depends on three elements. Firstly, there is the game. Secondly, there is the host. And thirdly, there are the contestants. We have a great game, he confidently asserted (he invented it!); we have an excellent host in Wayne Cox; so quality control rests on the third element, our contestants. Which is how and why we set up a school for game show contestants, where they learned how to play the game effectively, followed by a visit to a taping in which we recorded multiple episodes. By the time they came on the show for real and they had been practicing their skills at home, they were ready to show off these skills, excited not so much over the prizes, which were mundane items such as kitchen appliances, but just the chance to be on television. To hype the excitement levels, we made sure there were lots of sugary drinks and donuts in the Green Room. Not good for the waistline, but a winning contestant on a sugar high is more fun to watch.

We did five seasons with 130 episodes in all. A board game was created for fans and the format was licensed in Europe. CBC executives were so pleased they decided to commission a "celebrity" version. We produced one season of that, but we discovered that the celebrities were not nearly as impressive in playing the game as the regular guys and gals who had been to our game show school. We only shot thirteen episodes of *Celebrity Talkabout.*

Talkabout's success meant that when BCTV in Vancouver was looking for a kids game show, Comedia was approached as "the experts." What we devised for them was *5, 4, 3, 2, Run.* The main excitement here was if you gave a wrong answer, you had a bunch of goop poured over your head. Kids loved it. We did twenty-six episodes of that format. People were surprised that a "serious producer" like Primedia would do game shows. But if you are going to produce that kind of entertainment, do it the best you possibly can. It was a fun time!

In 1989, Comedia had a chance to produce a US Network special for ABC on Andrew Lloyd Webber's latest hit musical *The Phantom of the Opera.* John McGreevy and I went in to CTV to pitch the project, bypassing their vice president, Arthur Weinthal (whom some in the independent sector called Dr. No), and pitching directly to their president, Murray Chercover, with whom John had had some previous success. Murray liked the project and agreed to come aboard. Quite properly Murray called down to ask Arthur to join us, then announced his decision agreeing to pay the equivalent of a two-hour TV movie price despite this being a one-hour documentary. Perhaps Murray was confused. Arthur looked shocked, but did not contradict his boss. On leaving Murray's office, Arthur told us we had pulled a fast one over on CTV.

The show was to be a recounting of the original *Phantom* story by Gaston Leroux, and we had proposed filming in the famous Paris Opera House designed by Charles Garnier. We wanted Peter Ustinov as our host, as Peter had directed operas on that stage and was the perfect raconteur for the piece. Alas, when we flew to New York to finalize details with ABC, their executive had a "great idea" and announced that ABC had secured the services of David Copperfield, the magician, who for contractual reasons would not be allowed to perform any magic! He who puts up the most money calls the tune. Had we had Ustinov, Peter would have written his own script, included amusing personal anecdotes and generally livened up our recounting of the story set in this famous location with its mysterious seven subterranean levels. Copperfield, flying in to the City of Light for two days in between engagements in Manila and Las Vegas, had no connection with the story, nor with us. We cast Heath Lamberts to recreate the role of the author Gaston Leroux, and John did a wonderful job, lighting the grand staircase after midnight each night (as the opera house was in use during the day) and discovering intriguing locations to enhance the TV special. But it was not our favorite collaboration due to the host we had been gifted by a jet-lagged ABC executive.

CHAPTER 15

DRAMATIC EVENTS

AFTER *THE NEWCOMERS/LES ARRIVANTS* I had vowed never to work with Gordon Hinch ever again, but never say never. By 1988 Hinch was trying to get started as an independent producer and commissioned a good writer, Grahame Woods, to write a screenplay for a four-hour mini-series based on Michael Bliss' biography of Frederick Banting, Canada's first Nobel Laureate. Hinch and his neophyte partner Joe Green had no idea how to raise the money, asked if I would take it on as executive producer. Eventually Thames Television's programming head David Elstein agreed to come in on a co-production. In normal circumstances this would be tricky as the only British element was the role of J.J.R. Macleod, Banting's supervisor at the University of Toronto, who shared the Nobel Prize with Banting (which upset Banting greatly). Elstein said he would be content to let this be a majority Canadian production, with the only British creative involvement being the casting of MacLeod.

There was an excellent cast including the brilliant R.H. Thomson as Banting and British actor John Woodvine as MacLeod.

I felt it was perhaps the best work of Primedia's favourite director Eric Till, but when the Gemini Award nominees were announced he was conspicuous by his absence. *Glory* won big at the Geminis, sweeping the other top awards, and every recipient acknowledged Eric's contribution. The best director award went posthumously to Harvey Hart for another Primedia production, *Passion and Paradise*. It was a terrific evening despite the snub to Eric.

Four-hour mini-series were in demand at this time, and the format became a Primedia specialty. *Passion and Paradise* had started life as *The Murder of Sir Harry Oakes*, intended as a Canada-UK co-production. Oakes, the richest man in the world thanks to his discoveries of gold in the Canadian north, became a tax exile and took up residence in Bermuda, where he was killed in 1943. It turned out that an American producer, Len Hill, was interested in the same subject but could not get anything written as there was a writers' strike in the United States. Len summoned me to a very fine hotel in Paris and suggested that we might consider a co-production, but things would have to be done his way. I indicated that we did not work as service producers: we would be creative partners or go it alone. This prompted Hill to declare that I would never find the rest of the financing: "I will deny you the United States," he said. I replied: "Then I will deny you the rest of the world." We both looked at each other. A pause. And we burst out laughing. We agreed to merge our interests.

Once again, however, the experience taught me that whoever brings the most money ultimately calls the tune. Our British-Canadian script was a taut political whodunit centred on the corruption of the tax exiles and their Mafia associations, whereas ABC seemed to want a romantic melodrama with more emphasis on the involvement of Oakes' daughter with a French aristocrat.

US network involvement did, however, ensure we had a true star to play Sir Harry Oakes. Rod Steiger gave a triumphant performance. Less satisfactory was the casting of Armand Assante as Alfred de Marigny, the Frenchman accused of Oakes' murder. The Brooklyn accent did not really fit. But Assante was a heart-throb and was what ABC wanted. We assembled an impressive supporting cast, including Catherine Mary Stewart as the daughter, and I particularly liked British actor Andrew Ray as the Duke of Windsor and Canadian Linda Griffiths as the Duchess.

ABC was delighted that we would be the first big mini-series to reach the screen after the writers' strike. We were the toast of the town. Then CBS scheduled a TV movie called *Swimsuit* against us and it won the day. We still had very good ratings and critical acclaim, but it was instructive to see the difference in how we were perceived in Los Angeles after coming in second. Back home in Canada, ratings were magnified because CTV simulcast the series, meaning that their signal was seen on both ABC and CTV. We were still the toast of Charles Street in Toronto, where CTV had its headquarters.

Our next mini-series was *Young Catherine*, the story of the young Prussian princess who became Empress of All the Russias, written by Canadian Chris Bryant (*Don't Look Now*) and directed by Canadian Michael Anderson (*Around the World in 80 Days*). Our star was the young Julia Ormond, who was a dream to work with at the outset but became more demanding as she aged in her role. Her excellent performance, as opposed to the trouble she caused, made it all worthwhile. We had Christopher Plummer and Vanessa Redgrave, Maximilian Schell and Marthe Keller, Franco Nero and Max Frankel, Reece Dinsdale, and on and on. A stunning cast.

Young Catherine was produced after the collapse of the Soviet Union in 1989, during the brief interregnum between the initial chaos and when the mobsters (and Vladimir Putin) took over St. Petersburg. A film production offering jobs could secure almost limitless opportunities. We enjoyed access to cathedrals and palaces, lavish costumes and sets, and former Red Army troops among our extras. We began the day with a cooked English breakfast. Everyone showed up on time each morning, and no worries about overtime as long as there was food involved. The loyalty of our team of starving Russians was such that the bulk of them came to the airport to see us off. They had never had it so good, and we were well served by them.

It was important to be open to forming new associations. In 1990 Nick Orchard, a talented Canadian who had acquired great drama production experience at the BBC, was looking to produce his own shows, and Telefilm Canada's Robert Linnell (who had worked with me on *The Newcomers* and *The Wars*) recommended Primedia as a Canadian co-production home. We met, liked each other and formed a joint venture, Soapbox Productions. Nick's roots were in Vancouver and we produced a teenage drama series *Northwood*, filmed in North Vancouver. We felt it was at least as good as *The Kids of Degrassi Street* and its spinoffs, and the ratings were excellent for all four seasons, but each year the CBC kept moving us to different time slots where they were having ratings problems. We eventually produced thirty-nine episodes, but Nick and I resented the cavalier way we were treated by the CBC.

My next new partners were Claude Héroux in Montreal and Annette Cohen in Toronto, the former to produce television drama, and the latter for theatrical feature films. My first joint venture with Claude, as Primedia-Heroux Productions, was *The First Circle* based on the great novel by Russian writer Aleksandr Solzhenitsyn, starring British actor Robert Powell (*Mahler, Jesus of Nazareth*). Broadcast on CTV, it was an impressive production, and at the Gemini Awards that year there were just two nominees in the category, *Young Catherine* and *The First Circle*, so I knew I would be picking up a trophy that evening for one Russian epic or another. *Young Catherine* got the nod.

Annette Cohen strongly encouraged my feature film aspirations, and together we formed Primedia Pictures. We produced two theatrical features, both fairly low-budget and with enthusiastic young Canadian writer-directors. Both were contemporary stories: *The Burning Season* was shot partly in Vancouver, but mainly in India, telling a feminist love story of a young Indo-Canadian wife and mother who runs away to India in pursuit of her lover. *April One* was shot in studio just outside Toronto. Based on a true story, Canadian authorities are caught in a seventeen-hour standoff with a terrorist at the Bahamian High Commission in Ottawa.

Since the two films were being shot at the same time, we tossed a coin to see who would supervise which project. Annette thought she had won the coin toss when she was assigned *The Burning Season*, but everything that could go wrong went wrong and it was only her amazing talents that got us through. Working with the young Indo-Canadian producer Amarjeet Rattan, she and director Harvey Crossland set off for India. In pursuit of authenticity, they found a wonderful castle, but it was a location with few suitable facilities and four hours from the nearest reliable communications. We later discovered that the location was in the heart of "bandit country." We built a temporary village to accommodate the actors and crew, but it was monsoon season and, in a terrible storm, the village was washed away. I was in Cannes when I received the call from

Annette explaining the situation. I knew we had to call in our completion guarantors (the only time I ever had to do so) and they sent off a representative to India armed with a satellite telex machine so we could at least communicate. But Annette, a self-described "Jewish mamma," was made of tough stuff. She received a tipoff that bandits planned to steal our trucks and equipment once everything was loaded. She sent out a lot of disinformation about our departure schedule, then left a day earlier under cover of darkness and escaped with the film and equipment intact. Meanwhile, with the help of producer Julia Sereny (later founder of the award-winning Sienna Films), things went smoothly on *April One*, directed by Murray Battle and starring Stephen Shellen and Djanet Sears with the superb American actor David Strathairn as the police chief.

For Annette and me, these two films were our introduction to movie distribution, where test audiences screened and rated the movies and we were then told what to change to make viewing more compelling to audiences. Both movies tested respectably, but neither broke out in theatrical release, and many more people saw them in their subsequent pay television life. Primedia also made a number of direct-to-television films, including two 1993 projects that both had a maritime theme: *Lifeline to Victory*, directed by Eric Till, about Canada's merchant marine during the Second World War, and a remake of *The Sea Wolf*, based on the Jack London story. On the latter film, reteaming us with director Michael Anderson, we had Charles Bronson and Christopher Reeve as our stars. Bronson had recently lost his wife and kept mostly to himself. His was a gruff, internal performance. Reeve, on the other hand, was in ebullient form. This was another TV movie for Turner Broadcasting.

Which brings me to 1994 and *Love on the Run*, originally called *Adventure Inc.* Producing series for television rather than one-offs is where one makes real money, and if this is for an American network, you make a lot of money. Many Canadian producers, me included, were in search of this pot of gold at the end of the rainbow. Aaron Spelling, one of America's most successful TV producers, also saw this opportunity and sent his vice president Gary Randall to the Banff Television Festival along with the Canadian producer they had hired, Julie Lee. They were looking for a company to produce a pilot, already approved by NBC, in which a former mercenary and bush pilot marries an heiress, and together they set up an adventure-travel business. Mine was the company Spelling wanted to produce the pilot. What I liked about the pilot script was that it was told in flashback, an unconventional way to do the work of exposition when setting up the premise for a series. This was a bold move. In the two-hour pilot, we meet the couple, now in business together, who are constantly at each other's throats. How did this odd couple come together? The story gradually works backwards, peeling off the skins of this onion to find out how they met, fell in love, and married. Bound together in this new business, they now had to work in tandem while doing everything possible to confound each other.

We were to shoot on a mountain in Squamish, north of Vancouver. Casting was a nightmare, as the network kept second-guessing us and themselves. Eventually, we had Anthony Addabbo and Noelle Clark as our warring couple, and our heiress' father was played by Len Cariou (*Sweeney Todd*). To direct we hired Ted Kotcheff, an icon in Canada for *The Apprenticeship of Duddy Kravitz*, but I knew of him before that thanks to his work for *Armchair Theatre* in the UK. He had real range, having directed a wealth of movies from *First Blood*, which launched the Rambo franchise, to *Weekend at Bernie's*.

We threw in everything but the kitchen sink to make the pilot work. We brought a performing bear up from California to real bear country, because the Californian bear could act. There were stunts galore, including crashing a plane near Boundary Bay airport. Once we were in post-production, NBC got nervous about the flashback format and insisted that we put the film into "proper" chronology. This eliminated what had made the script interesting in the first place. Unsurprisingly, we were not picked up. Instead, the Canadian company that broke through with a US hit show was Robert Lantos' Alliance, which sold *Due South* to CBS.

A main source of Primedia's programming was still documentary, which is where I had started my career. Primedia continued the Gerald Durrell franchise I had started back in the Nielsen-Ferns years and developed under Torstar. One of our last trips to Russia under the Soviet regime was with Gerry in search of endangered species. What I had not anticipated was that the species in question were gathered in militarily sensitive areas (such as Siberia, the Kamchatka Peninsula, the Polish border). I am sure the Soviets thought we were part of a CIA plot and their first response was to offer us the chance to shoot in the Moscow Zoo and one other non-controversial location. This time I said *nyet* and the negotiations went on. Eventually I got all but one of the locations we requested. And, as planned, they got a little more money.

My final Durrell outing was a one-hour special called *Durrell's Ark*. The BBC raided its Durrell archive, and I mine, to pay final tribute to an extraordinary visionary who had dedicated his life to conservation, and specifically to breeding endangered species in captivity for later release into the wild. I had known Gerry through two marriages and a liver transplant. He drank prodigiously and loved a good meal. He could be ornery and difficult or charming and inventive. But for all his strengths and weaknesses, he always tried to do good and to make a difference. Who could ask for more?

Princess Anne, the Patron of the Jersey Wildlife Preservation Trust, agreed to appear in *Durrell's Ark.* I interviewed her at Buckingham Palace. She was engaging and thoroughly professional. She arrived at the appointed hour, spent five minutes chatting with the crew, and then we got down to business. She had done her homework and I got exactly what I wanted. When we finished, she thanked everyone on the crew individually and then took her leave.

And then there was Princess Anne's brother Edward, Earl of Wessex and now Duke of Edinburgh. It was my practice to take colleagues to various markets and festivals I attended, as it was a way to expand their knowledge of the industry. Prince Edward had asked for a meeting the previous year at MIPCOM. He was an emerging independent producer hoping to sell his stories to Channel Four and others. My first meeting was in the bar at the Majestic Hotel, a favourite haunt for filmmakers from lunch onward, but completely empty that morning save for a suspicious-looking character standing in one corner. I deduced that he was Edward's security. The Prince entered. He wanted to know more about co-production and had heard that I was an expert. His questions were intelligent, but I got the impression that some of the advice he had been given was what people thought he wanted to hear rather than the real goods. I had nothing at stake, so I told him some hard truths. He seemed to respect that and asked me to visit him in his offices in Charlotte Street in London. When I did, I could tell that his overhead was well above what a small independent producer could sustain. He had wide-ranging aspirations, but broadcasters only wanted him to deal with royal themes. It was hard for him to break out.

We met again a few months later when he was once more in Cannes. I invited him to lunch at the Gray D'Albion with my executive assistant Cheryl Knapp and me. He arrived with his security man and informed us that he had decided to forego his Charlotte Street digs, and cleverly was moving outside the M25, which would make him eligible for various benefits as a "regional producer." We never found a project where we could marry our efforts, but Cheryl did meet a Prince (though not her prince). Edward became more and more trapped in royal subjects. When these were historical, he was safe, but once he started a project on the current family, he was firmly told that he could not continue in this line of work. He was recalled to royal duties.

One remembers different aspects of one's productions, and my most vivid memory of *The Life Revolution*, a six-part series on genetic engineering, was the pitch. I was scheduled to meet at MIP-TV in Cannes with Channel Four's commissioning editor, John Ranelagh, and ended up spending virtually the whole week of the market in bed with a fever. The weather that week was torrential rain and the meeting with Ranelagh was a forty-five-minute walk from my hotel. I dragged myself out of bed, took a couple of Tylenol, and trudged through the rain to meet Ranelagh in the hotel bar. I thought I would die, but I made the pitch and he liked it. *The Life Revolution* got made, winning the British Academy for the Advancement of Science's Award as the best television show of the year, and Ranelagh and I became good friends. He had once written a history of the CIA and was clearly well connected in that community. Once, we were visiting Beijing together and the weather was freezing, John called one of his "connections" and was delivered a Chinese army greatcoat when we returned to our hotel!

I had always been an admirer of Dr. Jonathan Miller, as a comedian (*Beyond the Fringe*), a television presenter (in our series *Cities*), and as an opera and theatre director, but I had not had any experience of him in his official profession as a neurologist. John McGreevy had the ambitious notion of us co-producing a six-part series looking into the acquisition of language, the complexities surrounding language production, with a special focus on sign language used by deaf people. This interest was contemporaneous with Miller's friend Oliver Sacks' book about deaf culture entitled *Seeing Voices*. Our series was called *Born Talking: A Personal Inquiry into Language*. John arranged for an elaborate set: a study filled with books from which Jonathan would conduct his inquiry over six episodes. It was an intellectual *tour de force* if a little on the cerebral side, typical of its home, BBC-2.

Another potential project came about when I was in Vienna to speak at an industry conference. The gracious host was Michael von Wolkenstein, the largest independent producer in Austria, and a great believer in co-production. He had just secured an arrangement with Granada in the UK to co-produce a series on dinosaurs. I piped up that we had some of the best locations in Canada for a shoot on dinosaurs and one of the finest museum collections in Drumheller at the Royal Tyrrell Museum. Michael was intrigued and introduced me to Rod Caird, who was to be his Granada co-producer. Why not make this a three-way venture: Europe, the UK, and North America? Our ambitions grew. Combining our forces, we persuaded A&E in the USA to come aboard, and they in turn had ambitions. Why don't we see if Walter Cronkite will host the series? Cronkite was expensive and his time was limited, only ten working days at $25,000 per day. We started out flying him to our locations on small aircraft, but Walter was not comfortable on small planes, so each day the aircraft got bigger, as did the cost. But the audience Cronkite delivered was well worth it, and we produced a highly illustrated book to accompany the series.

My co-producers Michael and Rod were each in their own way extraordinary people, the former a Count and the latter (for a time) a Communist. While attending Cambridge in 1970, Rod had been arrested at an anti-fascist demonstration following some minor disturbances, and in the infamous Garden House trial, he was sentenced to eighteen months in prison. He put the time to productive use writing his book *A Good and Useful Life.* Count von Wolkenstein had all the trappings of aristocracy, and flew his own plane, often to North America to keep his pilot hours up. Generous to a fault, I once asked if he could get me tickets to the Vienna State Opera's Zeffirelli production of *Carmen* with Agnes Baltsa. It was already sold out, but he assured me he could deliver. We got closer and closer to the time of the performance and at last he called to tell me to go to the box office and mention his name. I did, and after some searching around the cry went up "Abbado. Abbado." Michael had secured for my wife and me two seats in the box reserved for the conductor's guests!

While it might seem like this type of partnership relied on happenstance, it was not just luck. When I went to Austria, I discovered who was who and made sure to be in the right place at the right time. I had to make my own luck, and be patient. I had had countless meetings with scriptwriters and read countless unsolicited scripts, but never produced any of them. Was this all a waste of time? No, because that was how I found talent. Perhaps a writer I met for lunch about their screenplay could adapt a property I wanted to produce. Without the meeting, this would never have happened.

Speaking of meetings, a less pleasant one occurred when I was summoned by the Ontario Human Rights Commission on the grounds of sexual discrimination, by which they meant gender discrimination. Primedia had fired a female sound person, and the OHRC's aggressive female lawyer accused me of a heinous crime, namely that I had fired a woman. She demanded to know why I had fired her. I replied that I did not fire her, the producer did. And "why did he do that?" the lawyer asked. I replied "*He* didn't; *she* did." After that their case unravelled. The replacement sound person was also female. Nonetheless. the OHRC decided to comc to investigate the company *in situ.* I asked my one male employee to take the day off so that the OHRC would discover nineteen female employees, doing everything from reception and secretarial to accounting and creative production. Had OHRC done their homework they would have discovered that Primedia had given more opportunities to women at every level than any other company in the industry. Secretaries had risen to become producers. Women had their chance to be department heads for the first time. We were pioneers.

Primedia had produced a series that was somewhat controversial with feminists, *Brain Sex*, based on Anne Moir's book that argued that women's brains tend to be slightly different than men's and that this might explain why there were more men or women in a particular field. At the time it rang true to me as an explanation of why I was hiring women at Primedia in preference to men, but the thesis has since been comprehensively challenged.

I was always looking out for new avenues of production, especially if there were incentives to encourage such diversification.

There was a fund to support francophone producers outside of Quebec, substantial populations in New Brunswick and Ontario being the principal targets. I knew the leadership of TV Ontario, and in this case Jacques Bensimon who ran TFO, their francophone channel. Through Jacques I met Claude Grenier, an Ontario-based producer-director who worked with his wife, a film editor. Together we formed a company called Les Productions du 7 Avril (the date being Claude's wife's birthdate). We developed a documentary series called *Transit 30–50* about mid-life and the crises it sometimes engenders. My companies at various times responded to such opportunities whether the incentives were public or private or it just made good business sense. The issues in my era were language, gender, and First Nations, and we certainly made a significant contribution in all areas, and these have now been joined through various cultural policies by the inclusion of LGBTQ and BIPOC incentives.

One of the best documentary series I ever produced was *Blood and Belonging* with Michael Ignatieff. It all started on a beach in Cannes where I was meeting Geraint Talfan Davies, the Controller of BBC Wales. I had nothing to pitch so we discussed the rise of nationalism in the post-Cold War world: Geraint talked about Wales, and I talked about Quebec. We agreed that a documentary series could expand on the subject and discussed the subjects we should tackle: Yugoslavia, Russia, the two Germanies, the Kurds, the Irish (but not the Welsh), and Quebec. I sold all six episodes to TV Ontario, which did an excellent job promoting and presenting the series. Rudy Buttignol, TVO's head of programming, turned the series into an event with studio discussions following the telecast of each film. Rudy started his television life as an independent producer, but successfully joined "the other side" as a programmer. After TV Ontario, he advised BC's Knowledge Network on its transformation, recommending that it get out of producing its own programs and give the work to independents. He was subsequently appointed president and CEO, brilliantly transforming its schedule and branding, and building a base of knowledge partners, donors who helped to supplement its appropriation from the BC government. But at that time, he enthusiastically promoted *Blood and Belonging*.

Michael Ignatieff was a perfect choice for host because many of these stories were personal to him. He had spent two years of his youth in Yugoslavia in Tito's heyday; his grandparents were Russian and owned an estate in Ukraine; he was a Canadian who grew up in Quebec; his adopted country was the UK in which a Protestant Loyalist community had been fighting the IRA for years. Only a man without a state knows what a nation-state means, and Michael could understand and convey the longing of the Kurds for a homeland. He was the storyteller the series needed.

Michael's strength is not only his dark and handsome appearance, but his brain whose workings you can almost see when he appears on television. This is what made him so appealing for me: he drew me in and allowed me to follow along his thoughts and his thinking. Michael is both articulate and very relaxed on-camera. But he also shares his emotions. In the film on Yugoslavia, he drives into Vukovar, the Croatian equivalent of Stalingrad, describing what we see and what he feels—complete devastation and buildings reduced to rubble. The continuous shot on Michael driving and speaking inside the car lasts two or three minutes until he comes to a stop at what was the city's main square. He gets out of the car and the cameraman continues the shot through the open sun roof where Michael, depressed by what he has just witnessed, declares despairingly: "this once was a great European city." The pain is evident. In that episode, Michael spends a night in a farm house where the farmer taunts his neighbour as a sworn enemy when just weeks before they had been the best of friends. Michael describes this as the transformation of the "narcissism of minor difference into a monstrous fable." Where once they shared fields, they now literally shoot at one another.

The book of the series won two major literary awards. Michael had already won Canada's Governor General's Literary Award for *The Russian Album* as well as the Royal Society's Heinemann Prize. I rather liked Michael's first novel *Asya*, a romance, though the critics did not: it was not what they expected from him. So, Michael wrote a second novel *Scar Tissue* and it was shortlisted for the Mann Booker Prize. That's how to answer your critics!

I had hoped to do more documentary series with Michael, but the lure of politics was too strong. He returned to Canada to fight for the leadership of the Liberal Party, but lost to Stephane Dion. After Dion's resignation in 2008, Michael became interim leader until confirmed as leader in 2009. He lost badly in the 2011 Election and resigned. I personally don't think he was cut out to be a politician. That requires an uncomplicated simplicity and a decisiveness that Michael lacked. He always wanted to get things right and would think through every possibility before he would decide. In politics, you don't have that much time. More importantly, as I knew only too well, when you have been away from your native land for too long, you are treated as a foreigner or an outsider. The Tories were lying in wait for him and they had him for breakfast.

In March 1993, given my interests and my recent work in music and arts, I became associated with the National Arts Centre in a call for the creation of a performing arts television network. In a presentation to the CRTC, NAC Director Yvon DesRochers challenged the cable industry to "offer Canadians across this nation some *real* choice—a national television service in both French and English, dedicated to Canadian music, theatre, dance and variety performances." We called it The Arts Network/Le Reseau des Arts and I was to be its Chair.

A hearing for new licences was called for February 1994. We were among the new applicants. Naively, we had budgeted to purchase all our equipment only to discover that our competitors planned to lease theirs. We made a change in these proposed arrangements prior to the hearing, and at the last minute were told that this was a "substantial change" and that our application would not be heard. We informed the Commission that we would re-apply, but by now the opportunity was gone.

PART FOUR

BANFF

CHAPTER 16

A PARALLEL LIFE (1981–1993)

ALL THE TIME I was building and rebuilding Primedia while lobbying for independent production, I was leading another life in parallel. I was president (in effect chairman of the board) of the Banff Television Foundation.

The origins of the Banff Television Festival lay in the 1978 International Festival of Films for Television held in Edmonton, which was hosting the Commonwealth Games at the same time. Alberta Premier Peter Lougheed was always an innovator and a supporter of the arts, as was his minister of culture, Horst Schmid, but the festival was the idea of film producer Fil Fraser (*Why Shoot the Teacher?*). I arranged for CFTA's annual meeting to coincide with the event, and it was a noteworthy undertaking: good films, good parties, and a good time had by all. Reflecting on this success, Fraser and Schmid saw an opportunity to build an ongoing event. Using both federal and provincial funds, Schmid recommended that a not-for-profit foundation be established: The New Western Film and Television Foundation. The new event was to be called the Banff International Festival of Films for Television.

Fraser hired Banff journalist Carrie Hunter to be its executive director.

A key player in its development was Dr. Jeremiah Ezekiel from Corner Brook, Newfoundland. Jerry, whose PhD thesis was on "Political Content in Commercial Feature Films," had originally joined the Alberta government as a film censor, thinking it would be a perfect job to watch movies all day, only to find he was mostly watching pornography and dreck. Jerry in time moved on to work in Horst Schmid's Ministry of Culture. Fil Fraser's book *Alberta's Camelot* recounts how he was able to get Jerry assigned full-time to the new festival:

> [Horst Schmid] suggested that I write him, requesting Jerry's services. I asked Jerry if he would write an appropriate letter to the Minister … Horst received my letter and sent it down the line for reply. It ended up on Jerry's desk. In the fullness of time the reply, written by Jerry and signed by Horst, came back to me, agreeing to my proposal. Jerry and I have since had many a chuckle about the wonderful ways of bureaucracy. He wrote two letters, both signed by others, which changed his life.

Jerry's prime interest was always the program competition, which he guided lovingly to be an internationally respected award, "the Rockie." Lougheed's wife, Jeanne, named the award and Alberta sculptor Roy Leadbeater created its physical manifestation.

The first Banff International Festival of Films for Television (later shortened to The Banff Television Festival) was held in 1979. There were 200 entries narrowed down to some 40 finalists. Various Canadian broadcasters supplied 9 finalists, and Canadian independent producers supplied 7. (One of the CBC's finalists was Bill Macadam's second series of *Connections*, which Dick Nielsen had executive-produced.) So, in effect, the indy finalists matched those of all the Canadian broadcasters combined. Three of these finalists came from Nielsen-Ferns, but neither Dick nor I were invited to attend, much to our chagrin.

The first festival was deemed a success, but in essence it went bankrupt. Thanks to the support of Peter Lougheed, it was given a second chance under the Chairmanship of David Leighton, then President of the Banff Centre, but only after a year's hiatus to pay off the festival's debts. Fraser's explanation was that there were two budgets: a real one and a dream one, and that Carrie Hunter was using the dream budget instead of the real one. Others told me that Fil's optimistic promises for sponsorship failed to come through. Whatever the reason, the event had been inadequately managed, and might not have survived had not Lougheed asked Alberta businessman John Burrows to join the board of directors. He was a huge asset, eventually becoming my vice president and in due course succeeding me as president.

The second festival was held in 1981. I found it engaging, poorly organized but with some homespun charm. I wrote my usual message of thanks, voicing some of my criticisms. Instead of telling me to "piss off" as I expected, Carrie Hunter replied: "if you know so much, why don't you join our board of directors?" I did. I soon became vice president, and when president David Leighton left in 1985 to run the Calgary Olympics, he asked me to succeed him.

Though a volunteer, I devoted almost half my working life to Banff, devising and programming the schedule of panels and presentations, inviting my international contacts to the Festival.

When I joined, it was clear that Carrie was the "heart" of the festival and Jerry its "soul." I guess I became its "brain," if only because I knew the industry in a way that Carrie and Jerry did not.

The board of directors was a large unwieldy group, but that suited me. Attendance by board members was so haphazard that I had significant control regarding policy and decisions.

Carrie had persuaded Gregory Peck to attend the first festival, even though he had little to do with television. While I knew we needed "names" to entice people to come, I felt that it was vital to have television industry players attend what was, after all, an industry event. International players needed to have their Canadian equivalents there to meet them. Getting the CBC and Radio Canada onboard was critical, and soon after that, both CTV and Global joined.

The festival was launched at the Banff Centre, but upgraded to the Banff Springs for a year in 1984. This revealed we were not yet big enough to merit that splendid location, though we continued to hold the Rockie Awards there. There followed a decade at the Banff Park Lodge after which, in 1995, we were finally big enough for the Springs, using all its convention space and the majority of its rooms. We had hotels all over town serving our delegates.

I soon realized that we never got the best out of the broadcaster representatives who were present. They tended to deliver the party line in generalities, and so independent producers had no idea what kind of programs broadcasters were actually looking for or what they would actually pay to commission such a program.

I came up with the format I mentioned at the beginning, "public pitching," in which producers pitched new ideas in public to potential commissioners. When asked where I got the idea, I reply that like many good ideas, it was stolen. I had read an account in

Broadcast, a UK trade publication, of an event the previous year at the Edinburgh Television Festival which seemed like a typically British attempt to pour scorn on the idea of co-production (especially "Euro-puddings" as they were called). At this session, British broadcasters pretended to be French broadcasters, German broadcasters or, heaven help us, Americans. They had a "make believe" producer pitch an imaginary project: it was dissected, dismissed, and a jolly good time was had by all. In contrast to the Brits, I believed in co-production and knew that at Banff we had real French broadcasters, real Germans, real Americans, and so on. And we had real independent producers with real projects. What would happen if they could pitch their projects in public? At last I could put broadcasters on the spot as to whether they liked a concept or not rather than letting them simply spew the party line. Furthermore, I could ask them what they would pay if they did like an idea. Complete with white board, I would write up the "commitments" we generated in the room to see if a project was feasible.

The first project to be pitched in this new format came from an Alberta producer with the wonderful name Wendy Wacko, so we called the session a *Market Simulation* with the sub-title *Wendy Wacko Goes to Market: Can She Make It Internationally?* Wendy said she had a surprise up her sleeve for me: she pitched a different project from the one I had prepared for, which forced me to improvise and perhaps added to the effectiveness of the presentation. To help me onstage with this and the other pitches, I had two experts, one Norman Horowitz, a distributor from Los Angeles and the other was BBC executive Roger Laughton, later chief executive of Meridian Television and chair of the Arts University in Bournemouth, for whom I had produced an episode of BBC's

Writers and Places. By popular demand the Market Simulation became a fixture at every festival.

The whole exercise was a form of reality TV, where the indy producers were the underdog heroes and the potential villains were the broadcasters. This might put pressure on broadcasters to look good and redeem themselves by offering commissions. Of course, I always prefaced each session with a statement that any deals offered in the room were not legally binding. Still, an informal deal had a moral authority which could be just as binding. Many projects found their first financing in this format; there were even bidding wars for a strong concept.

There were other ways to make the format more fun. One year I paired as my on-stage advisors Norman Horowitz and Patrick Dromgoole, chairman of the UK's private broadcaster HTV. They proved to have a comic chemistry based mainly on abusing each other's nationality. Audiences loved it and they became a fixture. In 1995 I came up with a way to make the presentation more exciting, placing the producers on the stage and the broadcasters on the floor, while I ran around with mike in hand to pressure them for responses. They did not always react well. One year, the CBC was offended by a couple of jokes made at their expense and I was blackballed, not getting any commissions for Primedia throughout the following year.

After a few years, the Americans heard about the format and invited me to present to the National Association of Broadcast Executives (NATPE). Soon after that, MIP-TV in Cannes came calling, and then MIPCOM, and in due course, MIPCOM Junior (Children's Programs) and MIPDOC (documentary) as well. Each new presentation led to more invitations. I was invited to moderate sessions in various parts of Europe, then in Australia and New Zealand, and even in Africa (at Sithengi). Then public pitching spread so quickly around the world that I could not possibly moderate all the events.

When Amsterdam's International Documentary Film Festival (IDFA) took up the format, they chose to do the pitching session around a table which in turn was surrounded by the audience. Their format appealed to the Canadian festival Hot Docs, who paid IDFA to license it—but they didn't have to pay me, as I had never patented the format.

I was recruited by the amazing Orna Yarmut to launch and moderate the CoPro pitch in Tel Aviv for Israeli and Palestinian filmmakers, which I did for the next twenty years. Eventually the Palestinians wanted their own event in Ramalah (RamalahDoc) with a video link to Gaza, so I did that too.

I brought pitching to Asia at the Asia TV Forum in Singapore, instigating the Animation *Superpitch* and to GZDOC, the Guangzhou International Documentary Film Festival, China, which I still host.

CCDF, the CNEX Chinese Doc Forum in Taipei, probably has the finest track record of any pitching event. Ninety percent of the projects pitched in its first decade actually got made. CCDF attracts Chinese filmmakers from the mainland, Hong Kong, Macao, and Taiwan as well as from the global Chinese diaspora. The year 2024 saw my fifteenth year at the helm. From that first session in Banff in 1985, almost four decades on, my format is everywhere … and I am told there are even university pitching departments with their own professors of pitching!

Meanwhile, in my real job, Primedia was at last making some impact in the USA. In the early 1990s Helen Fisher's book *Anatomy Of Love: A Natural History of Mating, Marriage, and Why We Stray* was all the rage. Fisher had looked at marriage and divorce in fifty-eight societies and adultery in forty-two cultures to explain the "four-year itch," an ancient human tendency to marry and remarry. Fisher concluded that we are moving forward to the past, returning to patterns of business, sex, love, and marriage that are closer to the way humans lived in ancient times. Primedia secured television rights to the book and proposed the series to Turner Broadcasting. Ted Turner loved our idea and we secured the contract for its production, which Rachel Low would produce and Katherine Gilday would direct.

After a lengthy meeting on the project in Atlanta with the Turner Broadcasting president, Pat Mitchell, and her vice president, Vivienne Schiller, I was taken aside and asked whether I would be prepared to offer them some advice on a problem project currently in production for PBS. The Turner executives felt it was flat and boring. After screening the fine cuts of this six-hour documentary series on *Pirates*, I agreed. My proposed solution was to turn the series into a drama-documentary by creating a larger-than-life on-screen character who would tell stories and narrate the films. I suggested Roger Daltrey, lead singer of The Who. I had just seen him give a spectacular performance in Jonathan Miller's BBC production of *The Beggar's Opera*. Fortunately Roger was interested and able to spare a week to shoot his scenes on short notice, so we rented a studio in Toronto, got Roger's measurements for costumes, and prepared.

When Daltrey arrived, I informed him that the script would be on teleprompter so he had nothing to worry about. His response had me turn pale. He said "I don't like autocue. I am a bit dyslexic." Had I contracted a rock star who couldn't read? Roger saw my change in colour and reassured me: "Don't worry, mate. I've learned the part." In a scant ten days since receiving the script? That seemed impossible to me, but it was true. He had learned all his lines and delivered them perfectly on the first take. I said we could move on to the next scene. "No," said Roger, "I can do better than that." He wanted a second take, again word perfect, and his performance was even better. This is how it continued for the entire week. I have never worked with a more professional performer. He told me he learned the huge part by having it pre-recorded and playing it back in an earpiece every day, treating the words as music and committing it all to memory.

At the end of the first day of shooting, I was in Roger's dressing room. As he peeled off his costume, his torso revealed the scars of stab wounds he had received earlier in his life, and I thought how different our lives had been since that time we both appeared at a Cambridge May Ball.

The stage adaptation of The Who's rock opera *Tommy* was playing in Toronto, and rather than rest, Roger insisted we go to a performance. I took him to the theatre in a Yellow Cab, and as we emerged I discovered what stardom must be like. The blaze of flashes from the paparazzi was totally blinding. I have been in many media scrums, but nothing ever like this. Roger was gracious with everyone he met, and after the show, he met the cast and congratulated each one of them on a fine performance taking special time with the lead singer.

A coda to my experience with Roger was an invitation to visit him at his Sussex home when next I was in the UK. My elder son Andrew came with me and we were treated to Sunday lunch with Roger and his family at his Tudor mansion. It was all very traditional: roast beef, Yorkshire pudding, roast potatoes. After lunch, Roger parked me with a cockney friend and took Andrew off to teach him the finer points of fly fishing. It made me all the more grateful to have had the privilege of working with one of the supreme talents of my era.

By now I had served my term as Chairman of the Banff Television Foundation and had grown Primedia as far as I could within the constraints of a tightening economy. However, the biggest constraint was a shortage of working capital. I had never taken on significant financial partners and was always concentrating on raising the money for one or more projects at a time. This was one of the ways in which I had been short-sighted. Unlike other colleagues, I had never built a distribution business or specialized as to genre. And I now know that I should have focused on making series rather than one-offs. I was enjoying life, but working much too hard, I was approaching fifty and could only go so far while still risking the mortgage on my home. But I resisted offers to sell the company, as I was too independent to contemplate working for someone else. I shared my problems with my lawyer Doug Barrett. Out of the blue, Doug thought he had a solution. P.S. Production services, an equipment rental company, had grown substantially and its owner Doug Dales considered Primedia a desirable target. I was a little too eager. I had always believed in equal relationships between partners, so I invited Dales to become an equal partner. I should have offered 49 percent of the company, for it turned out there was no way for two business partners to be equal when one has no cash and the other has loads of it. The one with the cash always wins. I had not fully appreciated the implications of the "shotgun buy/sell" clause in our contract. Unfortunately, lawyer Doug Barrett represented both sides of the transaction. He was keen to do the deal (and I suppose earn the fees) and suggested that we each could retain independent counsel at the end "to bless the deal." At last, I thought the company could repay my personal loan to the company and I could retire my mortgage. Dales and I went ahead and announced our "marriage."

The deal eventually closed, but Dales squeezed me hard on the terms. I was forced to break a lease I had just signed with my landlord, Ron Hastings, my Canadian distributor, and move to CineVillage where PS was located; Dales became more interventionist with both me and the head of another production company he was buying; and he asked me to mentor a young woman, Pam Davenport, who seemed to have Dales' ear in a way I did not. He then made her vice president of production and hired a VP of creative affairs for Primedia. I became desperately unhappy and realized that I had made a huge mistake.

I approached Dales and offered to pay him back all the money I had received from him. He refused and pointed to the "shotgun buy/sell" clause in our contract. In this arrangement, if I wanted to break up the partnership, I had to offer to buy him out, and he had the right to either accept, or take over the entire company by paying one dollar more than my offer. I complained to Doug Barrett who recommended I now take independent counsel. He suggested a friend of his, a nice man but not known for being tough. I decided to retain Michael Levine, who had represented Dick and me in the early days of Primedia. He was certainly no "milquetoast," rather the reverse, and that move either angered or frightened Barrett, who, I was told, might have to employ his own counsel as his role in the whole business (representing both sides) was ethically dubious. With assistance from Michael Levine and Richard Leworthy who had flown to Toronto to support me, I put together the best deal I could, but it was not enough. Dales put an extra dollar on the table and Primedia was all his. Ron Hastings told me that a single sale of one of the mini-series from my catalogue had been sufficient to cover Dales' outlay.

I had been outmanoeuvred. I finished *Anatomy of Love* under contract to Primedia, and then I was once more on my own. Pam Davenport, despite no distribution experience, was given the Primedia catalogue to manage and represent, so 400 hours of prime Canadian content slipped from my grasp, just as the Nielsen-Ferns catalogue had slipped through Dick's and my fingers into the hands of Torstar. I no longer had ownership in anything I had ever produced. Needless to say, Primedia's product slid from view until it eventually was given to a proper distribution company, but by then it was much too late.

A postscript to the story is that almost a couple of decades later, the Canada Media Fund launched a service, broadcasting quality Canadian programs via YouTube. It was called *encore plus media.* Its excellent head Paulina Arbaca-Cantin contracted to show a couple of mini-series I produced after the demise of Primedia. I suggested she go back to try to repatriate some of my work from Torstar and from the Dales Estate. She managed to rescue *The Wars* and *Karen Kain: Ballerina* from Torstar and persuaded Dales' sons to license ten titles from the Primedia catalogue, including *Billy Bishop Goes to War* and *Heaven on Earth.* Happily, some of my work enjoyed a second life and selfishly I could now for the first time get reasonable screening copies of my own work for my private viewing. A happy ending to a sad tale. Or so I thought. At the premiere screening of the restored and re-mastered 4K launch of *The Wars*, which I introduced at TIFF's Bell Lightbox on Remembrance Day 2022, Paulina shared the news that *encore plus media* was to be shuttered. However, I was pleased to have eleven of Dick Nielsen's family—children and grandchildren—at the screening of his magnificent achievement. We must preserve our heritage before it is lost forever.

CHAPTER 17

INTERREGNUM (1993–1994)

AFTER LOSING PRIMEDIA, I did not spend as long reflecting as I should have done. Instead I launched a new company, *pat ferns productions limited* (all italicized and fashionably in lower case), rented office space near my home, and jumped into a development deal with Robert Lantos at Alliance. But despite having only one assistant, I tried to carry on as if I was still running a company with twenty employees. I took on more projects than I could handle and almost worked myself to death. I had not learned my lesson. However, I helped launch a terrific seven-part documentary series based on the book *The Fifties* by David Halberstam; I convinced the producer, Alex Gibney, to move from Los Angeles to Toronto and become a landed immigrant in order to secure the funding. Alex remained in Canada for a few years and then moved to New York where his company Jigsaw continues to make award-winning series. By 2010 *Esquire Magazine* was calling Alex "the most important documentarian of our time."

While I was searching for new directions, Dick Nielsen and I reconnected with a view to writing a book together. The federal government was recruiting another commission of enquiry about Canadian film and television, and it was likely to go the way of all the other enquiries, never really addressing the purpose of public service intervention in broadcasting and film. Dick and I felt there was a need for some new thinking. Government involvement in the broadcasting industry had led to a proliferation of government initiatives that had come to dominate Canada's cultural life; we estimated that the government had spent $15 billion in the 1980s. We wanted to do a real review of the effectiveness of these policies and their side effects.

Dick and I called for a reassessment of the mandate of the CRTC, whose attempts to shield the broadcasters from normal commercial pressures had been threatened by technological change and consumer resistance, just as we had predicted years ago. We questioned the usefulness of the NFB, argued for a massive reorganization of the CBC, and placed our hopes on Telefilm Canada, soon to be merged with the Cable Fund to create what became the Canada Media Fund. We considered this the cultural agency with the most potential to promote the arts in Canada. We noted that the first thing Jeremy Isaacs did when he took charge of the newly created Channel Four in the UK back in 1981 was to limit administrative costs to 10 percent. What if this applied to Canada's bureaucracies? Put the money into programs through genuine creative competition.

Dick and I wanted to place these thoughts on the record. We had managed to shape public policy to a considerable extent, but there was more that needed to be done. However, in 1995, I found myself with an opportunity to really make a difference.

CHAPTER 18

MR. BANFF (1995–2004)

AFTER I HAD STEPPED down from the Banff Board, Carrie Hunter and Jerry Ezekiel had switched jobs, as Carrie had wanted to move to Vancouver. Jerry was president and Carrie one of his vice presidents. After the 1994 festival, Carrie, out of the blue, wrote a memo to the Board criticizing Jerry's leadership. It was clear their partnership was over. I learned that Jerry was advertising for a paid vice president of the festival, a role that incorporated many of the tasks I had done as a volunteer. The chance seemed too good to be true. I called Jerry to make sure he would be comfortable with me applying for the job. He was surprised, but all in favour. I was eventually hired, with a modest salary that was just enough to cover my Toronto office leases. Also, I had to pay my own travel back and forth to Toronto to supervise *The Fifties*. It almost felt as if I were still a volunteer. Nonetheless, I was happier than I had been for ages. I was doing something I loved. And Jerry and I worked well together.

It is important to understand the difference between a festival, a market, and a conference. A festival is a competition, usually involving prizes. A market is where finished programs are bought and sold. And a conference is where industry issues are analyzed and discussed. Banff was all three in one package.

The Rockie Awards were the central and defining element in our event, and it was critical that we attracted the best programs and that our awards were the gold standard. Our corporate awards enabled our delegates to see and hear from the top executives and producers in the world.

Banff was not a market in the sense of NATPE, MIP-TV, and the like, though some buyers came to find high quality programming which the Rockie Awards attracted and these individuals either "lived in the screening room" or stayed in their hotel rooms to watch our offerings on cable. Rather, we described Banff as a "marketplace of ideas" where producers could pitch new projects and network with the dozens of key decision-makers from around the global industry.

The conference aspect was something I held dear. We wanted the best minds to talk about our medium. Getting that done meant doing a lot of preparation: we needed to make sure that the panels were balanced and had the right interviewers; master classes needed appropriate clips to showcase the master's work. This is where industry issues, both Canadian and global, were debated: the decline of traditional broadcasters, the rise of cable, specialty services and pay, in addition to exploring our digital future.

I was only in my first year as VP when Jerry proposed that he and I switch positions, with me becoming president and CEO. This arrangement had to be approved at the next board meeting. Jerry and I attended the first part, but were then asked to leave and await the board's blessing … or not. We adjourned to the bar. Jerry's favourite tipple was a double Ballentyne's on ice. Three double whiskeys later I was summoned back into the meeting and unexpectedly asked to present my plans for how this new arrangement would work. I have no recollection of what I said, but board members in attendance said it was "amazingly relaxed, improvisational and reasonably coherent." It worked. I was now, in 1996, the president and CEO of an organization I loved.

Early in my term, I realized the need for a smaller Board of Directors while adding a Board of Governors (to replace the International Advisors I had brought in during my earlier association with Banff) so that we could enjoy the benefits of a big tent and the prestige of having some of the world's senior media executives on our "letterhead" as it were. When initiating the Board of Governors, I had much useful advice from John Hendricks, the founder of Discovery.

He told me I had to insist on having the number one person in each organization and that one should not accept substitutes at Governors' events. We had a Governors' dinner at NATPE (then in January) in the USA, during MIP-TV (in April) in Cannes as well as at the Festival itself (in June). These were mainly social events so that senior figures could network at their own level.

I was blessed with two excellent Chairs of the Board of Directors (Arthur Weinthal, vice president of CTV, and subsequently Trina McQueen, president of Discovery and then of CTV). As Hendricks had warned, once one steps down a level, the problems emerge. Thus far I had been able to enjoy the wisdom and counsel of the likes of Ron Osborne (Maclean Hunter) and Jay Switzer (CHUM), who could take one glance at a balance sheet and pinpoint potential problems. And they would do this in a quiet and unobtrusive way and I made sure that these "problems" had been dealt with by the time the next Board Meeting took place. After the term of such "top people" it became more and more difficult to attract *la crème de la crème.*

When running an annual event, in which people commit time and money to enjoy real benefits, you must provide for their needs. I understood that stability of expectations would be important: delegates must know in advance what is happening and when. For each of them it was a substantial financial investment and every minute of their time was precious. Delegates could not be expected to "learn" a new festival schedule each year. I wanted predictability with surprises!

One such predictable surprise was the decision to hold the Rockie Awards early in the festival rather than, as is tradition at most such gatherings, at the end. This scheduling choice ensured that potential winners would come to the festival right at the beginning. We played significant excerpts from all the nominated films during the ceremony to whet delegates' appetites to screen the programs that interested them. Later in my tenure, we became able to run the shows on cable, initially at the festival hotels and in due course throughout the town. It turned out that our "prime time" was in the early hours of the morning, as we kept our delegates busy with lots of events from morning to night.

I had added awards for corporations—one creative and the other technical (the first two winners were Granada Television from the UK and Sony from Japan). These were presented on Wednesday evening. Thursday evening was the Alberta Barbecue, one of the more alcoholic events in the history of creation, which we would recover from the next afternoon at Lake Louise. Blame the hard liquor at the open bar. After the RCMP arrested a number of international guests for Driving Under the Influence, we banned cars for the barbecue and bussed everyone to the site where the donut tents (circular structures with a blazing fire at the centre and picnic tables fanning out to the edges) welcomed the crowd. Sides of beef were carried on pitchforks to be carved for the delegates. There was a country music band and delegates learned line dancing. The greatest such evening was when we presented k.d. lang and the Reclines. Everyone was standing on the picnic tables to get a better view. Right after the show I asked our entertainment coordinator whether we had an option on bringing k.d. back the next year. We did have such an option, but chose not to try to enforce it as within twelve months k.d. had broken out on the international stage. She was huge. But that legendary performance became part of festival lore.

Another challenge for an annual event is the expansion of helpers as the festival approaches and the rapid contraction after it finishes. We had many returning volunteers, but even so we had to train 150 new people each year. My solution was to expand the number of events we operated so that I could add to the permanent staff. By 2004 we had almost forty employees and we were managing five other events around the world in addition to the festival. Twice a year we presented our week-long leadership training courses.

The year 1999 was Banff's twentieth anniversary and my fifth as a member of the staff. Looking at the anniversary brochure brought back many memories and a reminder of how far we had come. Our Grand Prize winners over two decades of the Rockie Awards had included programs in many different genres from at least seven countries, and our individual awards had gone to a who's who of television stars, creators, and innovators from around the world. The festival had truly global stature. The US publication *Entertainment Weekly* wrote: "the movies have Cannes, television has Banff." This was echoed by Italy's *Corriere della Sera*: "Nel mondo televisivo, Banff e considerato l'equivalente del Festivale cinemagrafico di Cannes."

I was happy and in my element at Banff. This is how I was introduced to readers of *The Calgary Herald* in 2000.

> Make no mistake, Pat Ferns is a major player in TV, here in Canada and abroad … [he] is known as the 'father of independent production.' … Ferns became deeply involved in the promotion and development of the fledgling Canadian independent production industry … his lobbying before the CRTC culminated in the creation of the Broadcast Fund of Telefilm Canada … He was instrumental in the early development of the Gemini Awards, recognizing excellence in Canadian TV … More than just a producer, Ferns has become a mentor, dealmaker and outspoken champion of independent production in Canada.

Trina McQueen, then EVP of CTV and recently appointed as chair of the Festival's Board of Directors, continued the description.

> He's always had an eye on the future, but to leave the warm, comforting arms of 'Mother Corporation' (the CBC) to become a television entrepreneur—well, it was bizarre at the time, totally audacious. He wanted the excitement, satisfaction and adventure of being his own

> boss, making films the way he wanted, living life on the creative edge. He's a producer at heart and runs the festival like he would a TV project—no detail is too small, nothing escapes him.

The culmination of her comments described me as "a true Impresario. He loves the stars, the sizzle. He lives life large."

Meeting some of our Banff award winners created memorable occasions, perhaps most notably when we presented the Sir Peter Ustinov Comedy Award to Barry Humphries (aka Dame Edna Everage). Barry was very particular in that he wanted to receive the Award as himself. He allowed that there was just a chance Dame Edna would come along for the ride, but no promises. When I heard from the driver who picked him up from Calgary Airport that there were numerous costume boxes accompanying our laureate, I was relieved. All our delegates would be expecting to see Dame Edna. Barry was receiving the award on Monday night and indicated that Dame Edna might appear on Tuesday evening if that could be accommodated. Of course, it could! I had planned a gathering honouring our corporate sponsors to whom we would be giving plaques of recognition. Would Dame Edna like to assist in the presentation. Yes, she would. This was not without risk, as Barry was known to be controversial. But I trusted that he would not go "over the line."

The evening started well. The first award was to BBC Television whose chief executive Will Wyatt was in attendance. Dame Edna made a few humorous remarks about that august institution which Will took in good spirit. When he went up on stage to receive his plaque, Will embraced Dame Edna and planted a kiss on her cheek. I breathed a sigh of relief. A lot of sponsors were in the front rows and I hoped everything would go off smoothly. I had not reckoned on Dame Edna asking for a member of the audience to come up on stage to assist. The President of CBC's young son eagerly pressed his case to be the one and Dame Edna obliged. However, she proceeded to explain to this young man her new project … to build a memorial to her late husband in Lake Louise to be known as Prostate World. It was hilarious for the audience, less so for me, but again Dame Edna went just far enough for comedy and not so far as to cause embarrassment … and the cancellation of CBC's sponsorship!

We tried to tailor our special guests' experiences to give them a memorable time. We had a police cruiser pick up Stephen Bochco (*Hill Street Blues*) from this private plane. Throughout his time at the festival, Bochco did what was asked of him, and then took off each evening with the RCMP to share stories (and presumably get ideas for future plotlines) in a local bar. David E. Kelley (*Boston Legal*) brought his wife Michelle Pfeiffer ahead of the festival for some rest and recuperation. We set up security so that if ever they were recognized in Banff, we would have a car pick them up immediately. Another superstar couple was Ted Turner and his then wife Jane Fonda. I sat next to her at dinner and told her about my working with her father Henry, who narrated a series that Nielsen-Ferns had produced with the *New York Times* some years before.

Walter Cronkite, with whom I had worked before on the dinosaur project, performed a magic act when he received his award of excellence. He arrived looking immaculate in a business suit, but when he saw a couple of guests in tuxedos, he gracefully disappeared in search of formal wear. The nearest rental store was twenty minutes away, but somehow he was driven there, fitted out, and returned in his tux in time for the ceremony. I still don't know how he pulled this off, but as with all his onscreen appearances, it seemed effortless.

Even more important than the famous guests were the partnerships Banff forged with other international industry events, co-developing formats such as *DocuMart* with Australia and *Two in a Room* with Sharing Stories in Scotland. Strands of Master Classes were added to the schedule. Canada's Embassies were engaged to promote the festival. Jeremy Kinsman was our first keynote speaker when at the Department of Communications, and then as Ambassador to Italy he hosted a dinner for Italian broadcasters outside Rome (in what had been Mussolini's summer home, given to Canada as part of Italy's war reparations). My daughter was travelling the world and joined me in Rome. The dinner was on her twentieth birthday, so Jeremy had all the Italians sing Happy Birthday! He later hosted a dinner in 2000 as High Commissioner in London attended by a galaxy of senior executives in British television. Other Embassies and Consulates from Sydney to Tokyo contributed to Banff's celebrations, as did the Canadian Consulates in New York and Los Angeles.

In the twentieth anniversary year of 1999, I suggested to the *World Congress of Science Producers* that they needed professional management. We were invited to organize their annual conference, which I had always found to be one of the best genre-related specialist gatherings I attended. This was because the membership was actively involved in programming the content. The Science Congress moved to a new location every year and our first time in charge was in Sydney, Australia in 2000. We decided to take key personnel from the Banff organization with us. The event went very smoothly and I thought we could create a similar event for history producers; science and history shows were immensely popular with the public at the time and a number of producers worked in both genres.

For the new History Congress, I decided to take my idea to Henry Becton, the head of WGBH Boston. WGBH was a big supporter of the Science Congress as they produced *Nova*, the PBS science strand. They also produced *The American Experience* which was the leading history strand on PBS and so would be predisposed to take this on-board. My relationship with WGBH stemmed from having been the first Canadian production company to have a movie (*Heaven on Earth*) as well as the first mini-series (*Glory Enough for All*) on *Masterpiece Theatre*, the pride of WGBH. Henry was immediately supportive. He recommended that Tom Koch, his head of distribution, be our liaison. I knew Tom so it was an easy relationship, though over time, Tom seemed to think the event was all his idea. We would launch the History Congress in the October 2001. The Science Congress was scheduled for Washington DC, so we would do the inaugural History Congress in Boston at the end of one week and move on to DC for the beginning of the next. (We suggested that delegates might like to spend the weekend in New York.) What we had not planned for was September 11. This was a huge disruption as many delegates were hesitant to travel following 9/11 and one reception planned at the History Congress for the tallest building in Boston was relocated to somewhere much less fearful. A cruise around Boston Harbour brought out extra police protection to guard international guests from terrorists. What we did learn from the back-to-back experience was that it would make even better sense to be in the same city for both events and to use the same Congress Hotel.

The next year we held the two events in Berlin, sponsored by German public networks, and the linked events were smash hits. The conference hotel was perfect with good conference space and a huge bar at the centre of the hotel where delegates could network. We opened the History Congress with a reception at what had been the Soviet Embassy near the Brandenburg Gate in what was once East Berlin. Many delegates (especially German ones) had never been inside. There was a big reception room dominated by the largest stained-glass exhibit I have ever seen depicting the Kremlin and Red Square in Moscow complete with a flashing illuminated Red Star on top of one of the towers. Had this been a set in a James Bond movie, I would have considered it over the top, but this was for real. The highlight of the Science Congress was a dinner-dance in the Reichstag, the ancient German seat of Parliament renovated with an immense glass dome to the design of British architect Norman Foster. One of the ARD stations (SDR) had a terrific Big Band so we danced the night away in the Reichstag. Most memorable.

Our success led to our acquiring other events. In Baddeck, Nova Scotia, there was a small, struggling New Media event that I thought had potential given the increased interest in the subject, so we acquired, promoted, and managed it, under the new title *NextMedia.* Given my interests, I thought an event for Arts Producers might be successful and we launched the *World Congress of Arts Producers and Performance* at the National Arts Centre in Ottawa.

During the period of my presidency, we were greatly enriched by the CRTC policy of demanding regulatory benefits from new licence holders whenever new licences were being granted or whenever existing media licences changed hands. Many of the so-called industry benefits were in effect chances for the broadcaster to invest in new equipment and the like, but at least 10 percent of the benefits had to be at arm's length and to be truly in the public interest. As a recognized charity, supported by the industry, we became expert at drawing from this well. Banff had CTV fellows, emerging filmmakers whose trips to Banff were subsidized;CTV funded $100,000 in prizes for *DocuMart*, a documentary pitching competition; the CBC sponsored the opening reception and the keynote address; Rogers sponsored the monogrammed bag given to each delegate containing the program guide and much else besides. Each sponsor jealously guarded its territory, and we had to be more and more inventive in creating such opportunities.

When Alliance and Atlantis merged their broadcasting interests, the transaction generated benefits for a new program for which we joined forces with the Banff Centre for Management.

The development of the Canadian independent sector had been achieved by entrepreneurs, few if any of whom had had any leadership or management training. Now these company CEOs were dealing with Bay Street and Wall Street and employing financial specialists who in turn knew little of the creative industries: it was as if two solitudes were struggling to come together. What if they could be taught a common strategic language?

I was placed in touch with Doug Macnamara, then in charge of Banff's Centre for Management, and together he and I developed what was to become the *Alliance Atlantis Banff Television Executive Program* (AABTEP). Our market was senior executives across the Canadian industry who might be dealing with megaprojects, or huge sums of money, interacting with Stock Exchanges and beyond; it would be helpful to offer a course that would open their minds to the latest techniques to build a business and an industry.

We knew that these entrepreneurs and their managers were very busy, so this had to be a highly intensive residential program of no more than one week. We treated our clientele with the respect they were due as senior executives. We held our programs at Buffalo Mountain Lodge, a resort with excellent cabins, gourmet dining, and a quality of isolation. And we worked them very hard indeed. During the five-and-a-half days of intense lectures, discussions, panels, simulations, and case work, often late into the night, candidates emerged exhilarated from new information, new friendships, and invaluable contacts.

Doug was the lead instructor and I was the industry instructor, with other senior industry executives contributing, each for half a week. Each evening the students would work on a real business case brought by one of their number, and then go to work on it, allowing the "owner" to hear differing perspectives on their case, though with confidentiality respected at all times.

I was very aware of the need to build a stronger Banff brand for the day when our regulatory benefits would tail off, and the need to find people who could step into my shoes if something were to happen to me. At Primedia, I never thought I needed a director of human resources, but at Banff I hired the very talented Pauline Martin to help me grow my staff in number and quality. I also responded positively to a suggestion that I hire an executive vice president so that I could focus on the future development of the Foundation, leaving the operational side of the Festival in strong hands. I saw that such a handing over would give my number two the experience he or she required. Jerry had been an excellent support, but he wanted to focus on maintaining the gold standard of the Rockie Awards, which he did in his role as senior vice president. For the executive VP role I wanted Jacques Bensimon, then running the Franco-Ontario educational channel TFO, part of TVOntario, who had ambitions that were unfulfilled there. He accepted, but then received an offer for the job he really wanted as chairman of the National Film Board of Canada. Jacques was an immigrant from Morocco and one of his first jobs was at the NFB. In many ways it formed him as a Canadian. I told him I understood that this was fate, and I lost a potentially great executive vice president.

With Jacques moving on, I turned to Jim Byrd, who had been an enormous help to the festival as EVP at the English Services Division of the CBC. One of the jobs I gave Jim was to manage the Television Executive Program, which he did with flair and accomplishment. I remained a member of faculty during our twice-yearly courses. Having Jim focused on the day-to-day gave me the freedom to concentrate on the future and to promote the Banff brand around the world. My biography concluded as a closing line "Ferns is married, with three children and lives on Air Canada." It was barely a joke.

As president and CEO, I had overseen the doubling of attendance and fund-raising, and established the festival as a truly world-class event. Indeed, its potential for success seemed to be limited only by a lack of working capital. With Jim in place as executive VP I could now focus on the one thing holding us back. Plans were discussed to retain the Banff Television Foundation as a registered charity and privatize the management, so it could raise money more freely. We were already managing several international events and thought we could take another step in that direction when we heard that an event for the news community, the European Broadcasting Union's *News Xchange*, was closing down. I thought we could fill the gap with a similar event called

News World. Alas, when the EBU heard of our intention to succeed them, they decided to hold one final event just ahead of ours. I should have cancelled *News World* as soon as that happened, but instead we went forward with our *News World* launch in Dublin. We split the potential audience, lost money and put Banff financially behind the eight-ball. This was our first market failure.

We had already agreed to sit down with Button, one of the world's leading exhibition logistics companies to discuss a merger of our management team with theirs. They built many of the booths at MIP-TV and other international events; we managed the content and logistics for international events. It seemed like it could be a practical and beneficial association. Then Button's board suddenly changed its strategic direction and pulled out of the negotiations.

Banff's twenty-fifth anniversary was approaching, we were losing money. The new chairperson was Loren Mawhinney, and I felt she lacked the strategic vision I had come to expect from her predecessors. I should have seen the writing on the wall the previous year when Mawhinney was chairing the board's human resources committee. Pauline Martin and I had spent a year establishing an elaborate system of performance reviews, conducting them and gearing our salary increases to performance. At the final meeting before the board meeting next day to approve our proposed salary increases, Mawhinney appeared to have forgotten all that had been agreed, said she didn't like what we were doing, and would recommend a small flat across-the-board increase for staff. There was no discussion.

Now she and I were at loggerheads. When the chair and the CEO cannot work harmoniously together and when there is no mutual trust, it is inevitable that there will be trouble.

And there was. I had a plan for substantial cutbacks in our plans, but Mawhinney would have none of it. She was out for blood, and demanded that I fire Jim Byrd. I said the failure of *NewsWorld* was as much mine as his and I would not fire him. If the board wanted him gone, it would have to vote to do so. It did. But I managed to protect Jim in the short term so that he could continue his work on AABTEP. However, I knew then that my own days were numbered.

While all this was going on, Banff was being circled by potential buyers, one of whom was Robert Montgomery, of Achilles Media, who had made his money in the dotcom boom. Mawhinney insisted on handling the negotiations, and I was dumbfounded when she announced that instead of my plan to privatize the management company, it was the Foundation itself that would be sold to Achilles Media, thereby forfeiting our charitable status. I then found out that it was Montgomery's recommendation that the Foundation declare bankruptcy so that his "new" money would not be used to pay old debt, but rather be invested in future business. I felt this was a complete betrayal of Banff's partners. Montgomery was now calling the shots, but he wanted me to "preside" over the twenty-fifth anniversary. I reluctantly agreed to his request that I stay on as president emeritus for the balance of the festival's year, but I would then leave the organization I grew and loved.

The new regime claimed that I was a "talented and respected visionary in the industry, but not an effective manager." Furthermore, they maliciously suggested I had lost the support of the staff. Jeff Brinton, Banff's director of marketing, responded to this claim in the *Globe and Mail* saying that "we [the staff] were totally behind him … The board approved every business plan and action that Pat took. Although there are some very effective and smart people on the board, the leadership was not there as it had been with previous chairs." Asked at the time to comment, I was ordered to explain that I was "in quarantine" and not allowed to speak out. But I did say, "you should await my memoirs!"

Five years later in 2009, Montgomery called to suggest that I attend Banff's thirtieth anniversary. I asked whether this was an invitation from him or just a marketing call. Was I a guest or a paying delegate? He said he would have to get back to me! In the end I went and was not much impressed by what I saw.

Ten years on, I was invited again in 2019, this time as an honoured guest for the fortieth Festival when the organization was again under new management and Montgomery long gone. Now the Banff World Media Festival is run by Jenn Kuzmik for Brunico, an experienced publisher and event management company. As I wrote to Brunico's CEO after that event, "Banff Is Back." It is once again in good hands, and going from strength to strength. Festival delegates advance or conclude deals and sales worth $1.95 billion each year according to a 2019 study by Nordicity. But this is no longer my story to tell.

PART FIVE

FERNS PRODUCTIONS

CHAPTER 19

FARTHER WEST: REINVENTION (2004–2024)

As WITH TORSTAR, AS with Primedia, I found myself in 2004 once more on the street and needing to decide what to do with the rest of my life. Jenny and I moved to Victoria, which had the most benign climate in Canada and excellent performing arts, and there I created Ferns Productions Inc. to handle and integrate a disparate collection of businesses that I had engaged in: producing, leadership training, and event management.

Though I did engage an assistant (the immensely competent Wendy Swinton), I found that in this digital world, real independence was possible. One of the few things I could thank Robert Montgomery for is that when he took over Banff, he gave me a computer and denied me secretarial assistance, thereby forcing me to learn to type my own work, which allowed me to operate independently in the digital age. I typed this book using two fingers, and "One computer, two fingers and three businesses" was my new motto for life.

In my new life, as in my old life, I worked on some projects that did not happen. Back in the 1970s I had tried to acquire the rights to make a mini-series based on Robertson Davies' famous novel *Fifth Business*, but an American film director, Nicholas Meyer, had bought the rights to make a feature film, which never happened. Now the rights were held by a Vancouver-based producer named Charles Pitts, and we tried to make it happen, but Charles had his own idiosyncratic style which did not appeal to some of our potential partners, and *Fifth Business* never came together.

Repositioning myself I had to recognize how much the industry had changed during the nineties and my time at Banff. I still wanted to find serious and important subjects attached to serious and talented filmmakers rather than "give in" to where I thought television was headed.

I was good at "classy stuff" but perhaps I never had the commercial touch that would make my fortune. Don't get me wrong, there can be high quality reality television, excellent docu-soaps and insightful life style programming, and the specialty channels were turning more and more to this fare. But it was not "my thing." For the true innovators there was a lot of money to be made. However, there were many, many more "hangers on" who produced mediocre work that nonetheless attracted audience and filled up the schedule.

Peter Bazalgette (now Sir Peter) was a British independent producer I much admired for his ground-breaking life style shows such as *Ready, Steady Cook*, launched in 1994 and making the notion of the "celebrity chef" a vital part of TV schedules and even entire TV channels; *Changing Rooms* (1996) spawning numerous similar "transformational franchises"; and *Ground Force* (1997) doing for gardens what he had just done for interior design. Definitely an innovator at the top of his inspiration, he had been persuaded to join a company run by two Dutch independent producers, Joop van den Ende and John de Mol. Endemol was just four years old, but Baz believed it would go places. He was right! They had a concept they called *Big Brother*, created by de Mol, that was immediately demonized by much of Europe. It was simply a logical extension of what specialty television, combined with an emerging twenty-four-hour around the clock internet, made possible. They would run cameras in a contained environment with a diverse cast of characters to see what would happen. Though the principal end product was the "highlights" that could be edited and screened on the main TV channel, there were enough voyeurs on the internet who would watch at any hour of the day or night to see if anyone was sleeping with someone else. In Holland, they were, so the internet audience grew and grew hoping for "some action." Just weeks after the series launched in 1999, Endemol received an offer of over a billion pounds to acquire the company. There was a feeding frenzy for *Big Brother*. But rather than sell out, de Mol loved to gamble … and he bet his company on the ability to make this work worldwide. He sold almost everywhere in the international market, including cracking the elusive American market: his future was secure.

Big Brother's biggest early success was on the UK's Channel Four and Baz was in charge of the production. He guided the expansion of the franchise in country after country, customizing as he went. By 2005 Baz was Chairman of Endemol UK and creative head of Endemol's worldwide operations. In his book *Billion Dollar Game*, Baz described de Mol as "the P.T. Barnum of modern television" who hit the biggest jackpot in the history of independent production. But he also relates the stories of two other UK entrepreneurs; Paul Smith who was responsible for *Who Wants to Be a Millionaire* (marrying TV and telephony) and Charlie Parsons who gave the world *Survivor*. The lives of these three individuals were intertwined: de Mol had tried to buy Smith's company before *Millionaire*, Parsons sued de Mol claiming that *Big Brother* was a cheap rip-off of *Survivor*. As Baz concludes "of this triumvirate of aspirants de Mol would make the most money, Smith would win the most viewers and Parsons would issue the most writs." Together they changed the face of television.

Those three shows epitomized what specialty television had achieved. A successful series in the specialty universe might transform the fate of a channel or even become the basis of a new channel. We had seen this with *The Sopranos* on HBO and would come to see it with *Mad Men* on AMC.

In the past, I had worked across many different genres and never specialized, but in my new life, I realized that I would need to find an area of programming on which to concentrate. Though I loved scripted drama, it had a long and expensive gestation period. I would do better to focus on documentary and particularly specialist factual programming. Mini-series were preferable to one-offs, so the question was whether I could find suitable projects of sufficient scale that they would attract a global audience.

On my travels, I discovered that the excellent New Zealand producer John Barnett (*Whale Rider*) was trying to get a Captain Cook project off the ground. His Australian partner, Tony Wright, was a friend of my younger brother. Knowing Cook's connection with the West Coast, I thought there could be a role for my new company. The four-part series was to be based on the work of

Vanessa Collingridge, a young Scottish academic who was acquiring a media following in the UK. With flaming red hair, Vanessa was a force of nature. We explored various combinations of financing structures and eventually settled upon a Canada-Australia co-production.

At that time there was an understanding between Australia and New Zealand that each would regard the citizens of the other country as their own. It made things simpler, except that nothing about complex co-productions is ever easy. *Captain Cook: Obsession and Discovery* ended up spending $180,000 on legal fees. There were three independent production partners, a plethora of film agencies, broadcast partners in five countries, and their financial rules were not always compatible. The master agreements between all these parties were so thick that each would fill a banker's box. However, things got easier once we could use the legal templates from that first production. For our next Canada-Australia co-production we reduced our legal costs to $30,000, and for my final co-production, with Germany and France, I did all the work myself and our legal costs were nil. That's progress. When we made the Cook series we had his journals to guide us but, of course, there was no archive film available from the eighteenth century, so we used an actor to represent Cook while a different actor read from Cook's letters.

Despite my intent to specialize, *Captain Cook* had come to embody my fascination with mixing genres, becoming a "documentary-drama." Our next co-production was what I would call a "drama-documentary." The true story was scripted and filmed with actors, but we included documentary interviews as punctuation throughout the piece. David Suzuki was our narrator.

Captain Cook: Obsession and Discovery provided a wonderful opportunity to work with my eldest son Andrew, who had been working on low-budget scripted dramas for a company in Vancouver. Perhaps his finest hour was in costume on-board the replica of Cook's ship *HMS Endeavour* in waters off Tasmania, directing the helicopters that had to film the vessel out of sight of land. Such was the skill of the helicopter pilots, and Andrew, that they got everything we required and landed their craft on their last fumes of gasoline. The visuals recorded that day are stunning. The series won the Gemini Award as well as British Columbia's Leo Award.

The series benefited from the contribution of the wonderfully witty and perceptive Mark Hamlyn, the key bureaucrat for the series at Film Australia (subsequently Screen Australia). Shortly after the *Captain Cook* experience, Mark returned to independent production, and became the co-producer of my next Australian venture, *Darwin's Brave New World*, a drama-documentary based on Ian McCalman's book *Darwin's Armada.* It was about four young nineteenth-century amateur nationalists, Charles Darwin, Thomas Huxley, Joseph Hooker, and Alfred Wallace, and how their voyages to the Southern Hemisphere changed their view of life and eventually led to the publication of *The Origin of Species.*

Another key partner in both these ventures was Hans Robert Eisenhauer from ZDF-Arte, based in Mainz. A serious and studious documentarian, whose opinions I valued greatly, surprised me when he revealed that in his youth he had been a long-distance truck driver. He thought nothing of driving two or three hours each way from Cannes to find the best truffle restaurant in France. Twice we drove around half of Israel in a day, ending up for a drink at the American Colony Hotel in East Jerusalem before a fast drive back to Tel Aviv.

Our second series together was mainly shot in Australia with a cast and crew drawn from various countries. Darwin was played splendidly by an Australian actor with an equally splendid name: Socratis Otto. We produced different versions for our different international partners to fit the time slots they had: for Australia and Canada we produced three episodes using mostly drama, while the French and German broadcasters received Andrew's preferred version, a five-episode series using more documentary material. This flexibility is only possible in our wonderful digital world. When I started in the business, we had to cut the original negative film, and so there was understandable reluctance to create alternative versions.

This adaptability became a major factor in my final co-production, *Listening to Orcas* (*Orques en Péril* in its French-language versions and *Die Sprache Der Wale* in its German versions). This project was brought to my attention by the highly respected French science producer Fabrice Estève. He had been approached by Volker Barth, a German specialist filmmaker who was conducting scientific research on the language of orcas and was confident that we could crack the code of their highly evolved communication system, or "Whale Talk" as we called it. Volker had very reputable backers in the scientific community, and this seemed like a sure-fire popular science program, but Volker, while brilliant, was a difficult personality who wanted things done his way. He was also in command of the research vessel following the orcas, and when it ran aground, injuring some of the film crew, it resulted in a year's delay as we had to film the orcas in the appropriate season. During the hiatus, the English-speaking and French-speaking broadcasters got together and demanded separate English-speaking and French-speaking directors for their respective versions. We ended up producing three very different approaches, all on one budget, and only the German versions focused on Volker's original research into language. Eventually, everyone got what they wanted, six films in all, but it showed me that after fifty years' experience in independent production and in co-production, I can still misread potential partners.

Outside of TV production, Doug Macnamara and I decided to establish something like the strategic leadership programs that had been so successful at Banff. We established an International Institute for Media and Television Leadership (IITL). Our first program was in Australia, where the CEO of Screen West, Tania Chambers, attended the course and became our biggest fan. Doug and I were commissioned by the Western Australian Government to consult with the industry and develop a new screen industry strategic plan. Then Tania was recruited to lead Screen New South Wales in Sydney, so we did similar work for the NSW Government. One of our IITL graduates was running Screen Territory in the Northern Territories and asked for our help. At one stage, given we were advising half of the Australia states, questions were asked in the Federal Parliament in Canberra about what "these bloody Canadians are doing." We clearly had a "secret sauce!"

Doug and I had developed the initial Asia-Australia Program in partnership with the Media Development Authority in Singapore, held alternately in Singapore and in Oz; we attracted participants from across Asia and Australasia. Europe was also interested. For several years, we had support from the Sachsen-Anhalt government in the former East Germany. We held the European event in Halle, the birthplace of Georg-Frederick Handel. Later we moved to Strasbourg where the biggest problem was persuading the hotel chefs that while we liked gourmet meals with wine in the evening, we could not also do this at lunchtime: our executives had too much work to do for a long (and boozy) lunch!

Then came the Global Financial Crisis of 2008. When the economy tightens, the first item that is cut from corporate budgets is training, and IITL became a victim of this trend. However, our graduates still gather from time to time, and we hear from several CEOs about their latest achievements, always thanking us for the skills they honed at our events.

Throughout all this, I continued to be in demand moderating pitch sessions in various countries and indeed to help establish or manage industry events. For twenty years I moderated Co-Pro in Tel Aviv, and I received an invitation from Guangzhou, where I have been doing their pitching forum for twenty years. At one point the state took over the event and a Beijing-based agency was appointed to manage it. I was pushed aside until the agency, Global Raytur, quickly realized that they had no idea how to run (let alone moderate) the pitching forum, so I was brought back on board.

A very fulfilling Chinese relationship has been with CNEX, a non-governmental, not-for-profit Foundation with offices in Taipei, Beijing, and Hong Kong, dedicated to furthering independent Chinese documentary. Its founders, Ben Tsiang, Ruby Chen, and Chang Chao-wei, had the idea to produce ten documentaries a year for ten years so that there would be a true documentary record of what was really happening in a fast-changing China. What surprised me was that the Chinese authorities did not seem to mind independent documentaries being made on all manner of subjects, controversial or not. What they were concerned about was ensuring that the controversial documentaries would not be screened in China. Hence it was important that we build international partners who would support such work.

What CNEX discovered early on is that Chinese documentary filmmakers needed training and entrepreneurial help in order to get these films made. Thus, they created the CNEX Chinese Doc Forum (CCDF) and asked me to be their overall planner and international consultant as well as the moderator of the forum, held in Taipei. During the first dozen years we tracked every film pitched at CCDF (usually 18 per year) and discovered the astounding statistic that over 90 percent of the films had been produced. This must be the best record of any pitching event anywhere in the world. After the pandemic forced us to hold hybrid events with many of the decision-makers attending on Zoom, it was a pleasure to be fully live and in-person again for CCDF-19 in 2023 after China reopened.

Another event which I was proud to help bring into being is *RomaFictionFest.* The president of Regione Lazio, the province which includes Rome, wanted a festival to compete with the Film Festival supported by his political rival, the mayor of Rome. I once again explained that the world already had too many television festivals, but I saw determination in their eyes. We devised an event that would cater specifically to producers of scripted drama, or fiction as they preferred to call it in Europe.

Planning for *RomaFictionFest* was haphazard, and the machismo in the office, where the men worked behind a huge wooden door and issued decrees to the women (and me) working at regimented desks, was the antithesis of the management style I believed in. But the Italians have a gift for improvisation just as they have a talent for brilliant design. However, the Award which *RomaFictionFest* would present was the ugliest statue imaginable: a male figure in a tuxedo with a TV set as its head. In the first year, the prizes included diamonds worth more than the cost of the event itself.

I will only describe one event, the opening of the festival in a 2,500-seat theatre. Twenty minutes late, a host came on stage dragging a microphone with a cord and started to talk in Italian with no simultaneous translation, despite this being an international event. After a while an old man came out and was given one of the ugly statues. It must be a Lifetime Achievement Award, I deduced. Then Jane Seymour came out and she was given her award. And her diamonds. No film clips to accompany the presentation. Then the entire cast of the mini-series being premiered that evening piled onto stage and were endlessly interviewed by the host with his corded microphone. Eventually, the cast was ushered off and the mini-series began: all three-and-a-half hours of it without intermission. It was about an Italian pop star who had committed suicide. The event left me feeling depressed. As I walked out of the theatre there was an orange carpet (we had orange because the Rome Film Festival had red) lined with pocket candles. I followed the carpet all the way to Castel Sant'Angelo and climbed up to the roof where a reception was in full swing. I looked out over Rome, the city illuminated to perfection. It was magical. The champagne was flowing, the food was magnificent, and by 2.00 a.m. opening night had been forgotten, and I saw that this could be the most wonderful festival.

Four years later our patron, the president of Regione Lazio, was caught in compromising circumstances with a group of transgender prostitutes and had to resign. Our fairy godfather was no more and funding dried up. Thereafter it became much more inward-looking and local, and my services were no longer required. But it was fun while it lasted.

Since returning to Victoria, I worked on a few films besides my own for or with others, including producing *China's Hollywood*, about the movie business in China, and *China: The Miraculous Transformation*, about the country's "economic miracle." The former gave me a terrific lesson in how the Chinese think. I was working with strong documentary filmmakers, yet the rough cut they delivered was a disastrous mess. What happened? I realized that they had slavishly followed my original treatment, which was intended a sales document and not a documentary script. Once I told them they were not required to follow the treatment, they did strong work and delivered a good film.

China: The Miraculous Transformation was a production for David Holgate and filmed as a series of portraits of entrepreneurs involved in the economic boom under Deng Xiaoping's leadership, mainly ordinary business men and women rather than celebrities. Though it acknowledged the vital role Deng had played, it was produced under the radar of the authorities so that we could assemble the film we wanted back in Toronto. Again, I was very pleased with the results. Having visited China under Mao Zedong and more recently under Xi Jinping, I had been wondering if Xi would turn out to be another Deng, but I fear he has become more and more like Mao.

I also executive-produced a series based on Charles Mann's excellent book *1491: The Untold Story of the Americas before Columbus*. The series was produced by Barbara Hager for the Aboriginal People's Television Network. Mann and I were the only non-indigenous contributors.

Though the occasional project still tempts me, I am now retired from production. I gaze out over the Strait of Juan De Fuca, watching orcas, sea lions, seals, and otters at play (or eating each other) as well as the maritime traffic of cruise ships, tankers, container ships, and even naval warships plying their way to the Pacific or on their return destined for Seattle, Vancouver, or Victoria. I can now reflect on a good life and a fascinating career. Few regrets. I'd do it all again if I had the chance.

CHAPTER 20

PLUS ÇA CHANGE, PLUS C'EST LA MÊME CHOSE

LOOKING BACK TO THE beginning of my career and the campaign my colleagues and I waged on behalf of independent producers, how far have we come? Yes, there has been a massive revolution in technology and there is a $12 billion industry to celebrate, but one must question how much the overall situation has improved. There are over fifty Canadian companies according to CMPA's Indie List 2024 that spend in excess of a million dollars on production and development. Just seven expend over a hundred million, and two of these are in excess of a quarter of a billion dollars. The industry is real, but dominated by giants. Almost half of Canadian independent producers surveyed are pessimistic about their prospects, because domestic commissioning of new productions is drying up at an alarming rate. So, we are looking to the international market to enable Canadian production, just as we did fifty years ago.

In her exit interview with *Playback*, the industry publication, Catherine Tait, the CBC President observed

> These feel like dark days. The industry is in crisis, there is no doubt about it. More than ever it matters to have stories originated from Canada owned by Canadian creators, controlled by Canadian producers. I've spent my entire career in this business and I think maybe I lived the golden years and I feel very, very concerned about this next generation of producers who may not have the same advantages.

In the digital age, the question is not only what tools are still available to support Canadian Content production, but which ones are still relevant. Some of the fundamental principles remain: the Canadian Broadcasting Corporation has still not found its way again and the National Film Board remains irrelevant. Private broadcasters contribute to the Canada Media Fund along with the cable industry, but these contributions are in decline, though CMF is to receive an injection of money from foreign streamers as a result of CRTC's decision pursuant to the On-Line Streaming Act.

The battleground for the future will be the evolution of our relationship with the new giants of content distribution. The tensions between commerce and culture are paramount. Can one marry Canadian stories with global reach? Will the new "masters of the universe" even want to try to help in this? Or are we destined to become their service providers rather than truly independent producers? Will the foreign entities operating in Canada simply make their regulatory financial contributions and leave it at that, or can they help project Canadian values to Canada and the world?

Of course, this is not a uniquely Canadian challenge. Nations around the world are seeking to resist complete dominance by the global technology giants. The lure of watching what one wants to watch when one wants to watch is pretty irresistible. In response the legacy broadcasters have tried to develop their own mini-streaming services, some more successfully than others. What is likely to transpire in Canada is a typical effort to "muddle through," hoping that domestic rules and incentives will somehow create some global winners. We should aspire to do better than this.

Independent producers are now an accepted part of the system, which was not the case when my career began. Broadcasters and streaming platforms look to us for creative content. But it is now much harder to build a company that can grow into a viable independent entity. Much better now to position yourself as talent and sell your services for a fee to the "big boys," just as it was when I started, except that the "big boys" are bigger than ever.

From the beginning of television, Canada was dominated by the United States, and in that respect, not much has changed. There are more Canadians in Hollywood, more Canadian performers on our screens, but the key creators as often as not are American. We live in a world dominated by Microsoft, Alphabet (Google), Amazon, Meta, and Microsoft as much as by Disney, Netflix, and Warner Bros.-Discovery, just as we used to be ruled by ABC, CBS, and NBC. A few more of our stories are being told, but we are under commercial pressure to follow global trends: more dystopian stories and comic book heroes?

What about the rules we put in place when we were building the independent production sector? There is pressure to revise what Canadian Content means in this brave new world. As Valerie Creighton, CEO of the Canada Media Fund, observed about the structures we built to keep Canadian culture from being swamped by our neighbor: "They were great structures, and they created an industry. They contributed to the GDP. They gave us an international reputation. But now the world is very different, and that brick thing we built is crumbling and collapsing."

In essence Canada's points system was an industrial tool to assist in building an independent production industry. It worked. From this foundation, over time, different institutions refined their interpretations as matters of social policy, cultural intentions, and how "Canadian-ness" would be supported. The points system delivered stability so that the Canada Revenue Agency could review with certainty what tax benefits could be claimed by Canadian producers and which foreign service credits were available to offshore production companies. But we are still engaged in an unresolved struggle, fifty years later, to define our goals.

The big question is: should Canadian content be defined as programs made in Canada or programs made by Canadians? The latter category is how our world has operated to date, but what about all those streamers—Netflix, Amazon, and the like–who are spending millions of dollars in Canada? Aren't their programs Canadian? How important should creative control be? If Netflix is putting up all the money, why can't it have the same controls that a Bell Media or a the CBC has over its independent production clients? All this will be debated, no doubt endlessly, but I believe a solution is staring us in the face.

Tax credit regimes have delivered funding to Canadian producers doing original work at a higher level than production service funding has been granted to foreign producers. This is as it should be. But then why not do something similar in determining Canadian content status? If one has Canadians in key creative roles, this should be worth more than if a foreign company is simply using Canadian technical resources. But all productions shot in Canada should be given some value in assessing (or offsetting) the amounts foreign streamers are expected to contribute to the Canadian system. The streamers should be entitled to offset some of the regulatory levy if they meet new Canadian content standards: giving them more recognition and more value the more creative positions Canadians occupy in their productions, whether Canadians hold profit positions from foreign sales, and the like.

Too much stress has traditionally been placed on intellectual property rights, causing conflict with Americans who are putting up all the money and cannot understand why Canadians must retain copyright in order to make a production. Sharing revenues is a much more realistic way to negotiate a deal than fighting over something that makes little difference at the end of the day. Canadian regulators and funding institutions should be more flexible, able to grant reasonable exceptions where more production is preferable to less, and more Canadian participation is preferable to less.

The institutional balance has always favoured protection from abuse by the Americans rather than the encouragement of Canadian talent to innovate and take risks. What we are striving for is a tiered system that does not reduce the amount of work for Canadians, acknowledges that Canadian creativity should be rewarded, provides increasing incentives the more that Canadians play key roles, and breathes life into experimentation. As the industry rushes to consolidate, I fear we are retreating to a project-by-project world of evaluation once again in which the little guys are being crushed by the big: 'twas ever thus.

The CRTC still regulates, but regulation is becoming harder and harder. The pace of its decision-making has been glacial, though in fairness to them, its decision of a levy on foreign operations under the On-line Streaming Act came much quicker than anyone expected. However, the real impact will come from its decisions on the definition of Canadian content.

Which brings us to the CBC. In 2004, it appointed Richard Stursberg, a former head of Telefilm Canada to the role of Head of the English Services Division. Stursberg observed in his book *The Tower of Babble* that he landed into a "culture of bureaucracy and apathy." He described himself as a popularizer and, before he ran afoul of the President and was dismissed, emphasized creating shows to compete with the Americans in their writing and production, such as *Little Mosque on the Prairie*. I agree with him that quality and popularity are compatible, but I profoundly disagree with his view that ratings are the key measure of success.

His regime and his philosophy brought us the return of *Wheel of Fortune* and *Jeopardy*. I still believe that a public service broadcaster must pay equal, if not more attention to reach. And still feel that the presence of advertising distorts the CBC's mission.

A dependence on advertising revenue means that the CBC will always pursue ratings rather than reach, and this makes it harder to differentiate itself from its creative competitors. The role of the CBC is in part to bind our country together. Show one region what is happening in other regions. Share perspectives. Find points of distinction. To this day the CBC still lacks creative leadership. The critical mass of talent in this bilingual country is in Toronto and Montreal, and yet for years the CBC president was based in Ottawa in a bureaucratic headquarters, far away from most of the creative community. I would advocate having two presidents, one in Toronto for the English-language CBC and one in Montreal for Radio-Canada. Give each autonomy, perhaps under a hands-off single board of directors. Each should be creative appointments, not managers or administrators.

It used to be said that the CBC's journalism would always rise above the rest. But if ratings are your test, *CTV National* outperforms the CBC's *The National.* The public network is where the public affairs of the country should be properly debated, but public interest will not revive unless its journalism does. Some hark back to the glory years of *The National* and *The Journal.* This was no golden age, but part of the decline: a period when Canadian documentary (one of our strengths) was replaced by "radio with pictures," a formulaic approach emphasizing shorter and shorter stories. What happened to the authored long-form documentary on which we built an international reputation? It almost disappeared.

The CBC leadership's perception is still that the problem is financial, and the corporation can save itself through an expansion of infomercial programming! More commercial influence, not less. They have it backwards, as I have been saying for decades. Less can be more, and in the case of the CBC it would be.

The state of the commercial broadcasters is not much better. *CTV National* axed its popular female host Lisa LaFlamme, drawing accusations of ageism and sexism. But CTV's owner, Bell, argued that it was just business. They saw audience demographics changing, and since ratings ruled for them, they responded by chasing a younger audience. As with the CBC, the leadership of CTV sees their company as an entity to be managed rather than creatively led. The commercial networks had to be dragged kicking and screaming into supporting real Canadian content programming: they could then and can still now prosper on their sports coverage and acquired American entertainment. That's not good enough. Global Television was created to serve independents, but unlike Channel Four in the UK, it has consistently failed to proactively support the independent community.

Pay Television did not bring about creative change in Canada as did HBO in the United States. A model based on subscribers rather than advertisers brought US viewers and creators the advantages that were already present in the UK thanks to the BBC: programs that did not have to be structured to appeal to accommodate the formulae demanded by advertisers. Canada, on the other hand, remains within the old TV ecology dominated by commercial interests which often remain unchallenged.

Even in commercial television, however, the quality of leadership in the UK has always been superior to what we had in Canada. Why? Because the leadership came from the ranks of the creative community, who had deep experience of making programs, and thus really knew their industry. I worked in co-production with various colleagues at BBC who rose to the top of that organization or other equivalent ones. In Canada, I might meet a CBC president when lobbying in Ottawa, but they were never a friend nor a colleague. We had never worked together. And none during my career were "of the industry." They were appointed for other reasons.

The National Film Board of Canada has a fine reputation internationally, mainly because no one knows what it does other than win the occasional Oscar for its animation. It has parlayed that small track record into a belief that it deserves to exist. When I started in the industry it still had credibility from its English and French feature films directed by the likes of Don Owen and Claude

Jutra, but increasingly I saw its logo jeered by Canadian audiences when one of its shorts was shown in a cinema. The essence of the NFB's problem is that it lacked real connection with the Canadian audience, which it could have achieved through exposure on the CBC and Radio-Canada. Making programs with no audience is the worst of all possible worlds. But the respective leaderships of each organization could never get it together. Independent producers know how to reach audiences, and producers know how to collaborate, but these organizations do not. Even the CBC and Radio-Canada find it hard to work together under a single president.

As for the quest to build a Canadian feature film industry, it was a quest destined for failure, certainly as regards English-Canada. French Canada has built a boutique feature film industry and spawned some global masters like Denis Villeneuve. What English Canada has to show are some individual filmmakers (Cronenberg, Egoyan) but no real sustainable industry of substance.

The main factor in the growth of that $12 billion industry I mentioned has been the Broadcast Development Fund. This was the tool the independent sector needed and has been supplemented with various provincial tax credit programs for both the creative sector producing Canadian Content and for the service industry. Most of the creativity is located in Toronto and Montreal, though British Columbia has become expert in servicing Hollywood. While it may be theoretically feasible (and politically correct) to have mini-industries in each province, it has to be accepted that, as in the US and the UK, the talent will usually be centred in one or two places. In moving to the West Coast as a producer, I discovered the disadvantages of trying to build a company there when most of the decision-making is in Toronto. This disadvantage of distance has not changed, despite digital technology. Face-to-face contact is absolutely key to success in the creative industries, which is why I spent so much time flying around the world to engage potential partners.

I often wonder whether it is age that now makes me so cantankerous. Or is this the result of a lifetime of being an outsider and the underdog? Still, I recall that when I came to Canada, Trudeau *père*'s controversial policies, from energy policy to the War Measures Act, were debated with professional journalistic standards on the public television network, as they were in the bedrooms and dining rooms of the nation. Now, the debate about the policies of Trudeau *fils* is reduced to "Fuck Trudeau." Journalists approach the Ottawa "convoyards" with deference, seeming to believe that their views have an equivalency with anyone who has received a basic education in civics. The kids may now be smarter, but they appear to have less knowledge, not more. As my mentor Malcolm Muggeridge stated, the problem in a post-Western European Christian culture is not that people now have no beliefs, it is that they believe in anything. The internet, not responsible media, purveys all manner of conspiracy theories. The legacy of Donald Trump and his fake news is that it is, in Muggeridge's words, "all true except the facts." Follow your leader and accept his "truth."

At the beginning of my career, people read some of the same newspapers, watched some of the same television programs, even read some of the same books, so there was at least some consensus at the proverbial water cooler as to what the issues were. Now anything goes. The best political analysis comes from late-night comedy shows rather than the traditional news sources.

And what of the pioneers? Michael Hirsh has been a spectacular success, though not without his ups and downs. As he put it to me, when a cartoon character comes to the edge of the cliff, he does not stop but keeps running through the air until he reaches the other side. Michael never stopped running when confronting disaster. He built Nelvana, sold it to Corus, and had the new owners been less cautious and more courageous, they could have conquered the world in pre-school programming. Michael then cleansed the assets of the fraudulent Cinar to create Cookie Jar, and now he presides over Wow! Unlimited. As long as he can keep making things happen, he won't retire. His wife Elaine is one of Canada's preeminent digital painters, exhibiting as T.M. Glass.

As regards Robert Lantos and Michael Macmillan, Alliance-Atlantis begat Entertainment One; then it became a creature of Hanna-Barbera; now Lionsgate has acquired it. Instead of operating in Canada as an American major, it has now decided to create Lionsgate Canada, re-entering the Canadian space not as small player but as an industry leader. Robert saw television as a way to make money to finance his dream of being a feature film producer, and he succeeded. Michael dreamed of having his own channels and so became a broadcaster. Having sold that on, he is doing it all over again with spectacular success as CEO of Blue Ant, a global player and promoter of FAST channels.

John Brunton took over the assets of Pen Densham's and John Watson's Insight Productions and made a huge success of working with broadcasters, especially the CBC and CTV, to create popular entertainment formats and long-running franchises such as *The Amazing Race Canada, Big Brother Canada,* and *Canada's Ultimate Challenge.* Densham and Watson are part of the Canadian diaspora in Los Angeles.

Bill Macadam retired to the family estate in Norfolk, where he lives in the gamekeeper's cottage, having passed the Hall to his younger brother's family. He protects the countryside and maintains an avid interest in the politics of the UK, USA, and Canada.

And I am left to my musings and to training a new generation of documentary filmmakers, helping them turn their dreams into reality.

The pitching, public and private, goes on.

CHAPTER 21

CODA

WHAT HAVE I LEARNED professionally and personally? I know that I have had a blessed life in both my career and in my personal life. I have made a lot of mistakes and know that there are many things I should have done differently. Much of my success was attributable to good fortune. Nonetheless, as the old adage says, you make your own luck. I have come to recognize that the key to success in the cultural industries is hard work, trust, and collaboration. I have had great mentors, and I have associated myself with talented people and then tried to stay out of their way so they could do their best work. And I had some analytical ability, knowing my audience and my market.

I believe I have a gift for friendship, and as co-production has been at the heart of my work, intuition about people and the ability to give and receive trust is paramount. My career benefited from my urge to be independent, from my competitive streak, and frankly, my addiction. I am now a recovering workaholic. I was compelled to show I was working harder than anyone else around me. Perhaps this comes from being a second son: as in the old Avis commercials, "we're number two: we try harder."

My main weakness as a manager was an avoidance of conflict. I rarely raised my voice; instead I would go quiet, and I was surprised to find that my staff often found this intimidating. If I could have grasped the nettle more often it would have been a better approach. A former employee of the Banff Television Festival was interviewed about working for me. Her assessment: "It's not easy working for Pat. He challenges your thinking, your fears, your commitment, yet you can't help but grow professionally under his leadership. He opens doors you never thought of and tells you to get out there."

As I observed at the beginning, I have always felt like an outsider wherever I happened to be. While this may explain a need to be accepted on a personal level, it did provide me with perspective that has been helpful both professionally and as an industry builder. One must have an ability to see context as a producer and as a lobbyist: to get inside the head of one's potential partners as well as one's adversaries.

Reflecting on the fight for independent production, those who were most helpful and who had most drive were outsiders like me: Bill Macadam, the Old Etonian/bush pilot from the UK, and Michael Hirsh, the Jewish Belgian immigrant. Like me, the Canadian expatriate, they were outsiders who became insiders. We all saw that co-production was going to be the key to building the industry and creating competitive work. But though my efforts with Bill, Michael, and many others contributed to the growth of a $12 billion industry, I still question if I am really part of it. Television is definitely in my blood, but do I really belong?

While I always tried to give back to the industry, I have been given much recognition. In 1990, the Academy of Canadian Film and Television made me only the fifth recipient of a Personal Lifetime Achievement Award. Such acknowledgment by my peers was humbling. But the most satisfying acknowledgment in my career was being made a member of the Order of Canada, receiving our nation's highest civilian honour from Governor General Michaëlle Jean. It was a splendid ceremony at Rideau Hall which my children Katharine and Mark attended with my wife Jenny (my eldest son Andrew was away filming). The citation acknowledged three areas of accomplishment: my role in building the independent production industry; the development of the Banff Television Festival to be a world-class event; and my body of work, contributing high quality Canadian content for the enjoyment of Canadian audiences.

Since receiving that award my contributions have been more international in nature, but all of them with Canadian roots. The public pitching format I created is now a world-wide phenomenon. I helped to build enduring international events such as Co-Pro in Israel, RomaFictionFest in Italy, GZDOC in China, and CCDF in Taiwan. Canada has always provided players on the international scene and the global industry has been enhanced by such Canadian contributions.

My dedication to this work, my addiction, cost me personally. Spending my life on Air Canada, I was frequently an absentee husband, and after forty-one years of marriage, Jenny left me in 2009. Reflecting on this after the fact, I can see why. She was a talented woman and had left her high school as head girl. But she was unsatisfied as a teacher and did not wish to work in my industry. Once the children were in school she did various forms of counselling and eventually took her Master's degree and qualified as a certified psychologist, but this too became unsatisfying. I was leading a full and successful life in an industry that provides plenty of affirmation. I was in the spotlight and she perhaps needed her turn in it. For me it was a shock when she left. I spent a brief time in therapy and came to terms with my situation. Jenny was my first and only girlfriend, and now I had to start dating, living life in reverse. Through online dating I got to meet a lot of interesting and intelligent women. I made misjudgements along the way, but my taste for strong independent women was finally met by the marvellous Carole Bawlf, who became my second wife. Unfortunately, she was diagnosed with terminal cancer a year into our relationship. I nursed her through her chemo treatments and she was eventually given an assisted death, one of the first in British Columbia. Though brief, I would not have missed those two years for the world. Carole said these were the happiest years of her life. Once again, I entered the dating scene and was fortunate to find my current partener, another highly independent, strong, and very successful woman. Yes, I have been truly blessed.

While I may have had deficiencies as a husband, I hope I have been a good father to my three children. All of them, as well as their partners, are artists in one field or another. Andrew is a very fine writer, director, and producer; Katharine is a painter and sculptor who also worked as a stand-up comedian; Mark is an actor. This is hardly surprising. The world they saw me inhabiting seemed exciting, they interacted with famous people and I made sure they saw something of my professional life firsthand. I took Andrew to see Hadrian's Wall when I was working with BBC Scotland; Katharine to P.E.I. to visit *Anne of Green Gables* when I was lobbying there; Mark to Los Angeles to visit Universal City while I was pitching American clients: and in turn they each attended *Just for Laughs* in Montreal where I moderated *Just for Pitching*. In Los Angeles, the whole family attended *Tamara*, the interactive play, where we each followed different actors and storylines throughout the mansion where the play was performed. We had great fun comparing notes during intermission. I used to joke that I hoped one of my children would be a plumber or "something useful." But, in truth, I am glad they have all found fascinating and fulfilling creative work as well as interesting partners with whom to share their lives.

Inhabiting a world of artistic endeavour is at once challenging and rewarding. I don't think I have ever been bored. And I have come to recognize and appreciate that my children are my only real legacy. It is to them that this book is dedicated.

ACKNOWLEDGMENTS

I WOULD ATTRIBUTE MUCH OF whatever I have achieved to the women with whom I worked. I believe in women's superior gifts of intuition, communication, and loyalty. I had secretaries that went on to become executive assistants and then producers, Cheryl Knapp being one. She was a wonderful secretary, and when I promoted her to be my executive assistant, we hired a replacement secretary, Maureen Dorey, who, like Cheryl, stayed for many years, ending up as a superb story editor. Cheryl became a first-rate producer with the Kratts brothers. Mary Ness, a long-serving receptionist (a key position, as they provide the first impression of your company) went on to be an artist and entrepreneur. Penny Hozy, a visual researcher, became an editor. Jackie Kelly went from bookkeeper and accountant to director of finance. Anna Newallo is a cultural bureaucrat at Ontario Creates. All are making an impact. And there were many more with similar stories.

I had several excellent female producers work with me over time, notably Paula Quigley who did splendidly on our Durrell series and married our English co-producer, thereby becoming Paula Harris. Rachel Low was another stellar appointment going on to create her own company in the factual entertainment field. And Ann O'Brien with whom I worked on *Stage on Screen*. In business affairs, former Telefilm Canada Executive Gwen Iveson was a huge asset as my Production Supervisor at Primedia.

My partnership with Annette Cohen for Primedia Pictures was a source of great joy. Some of my greatest satisfactions were to give head of department opportunities to women who had previously been number two to a male HOD. *Heaven on Earth* was one such production featuring numerous such appointments, all at one time, and each of these women rose to the occasion.

It started early with teachers who made an impression: Miss Fenn in Junior School had me writing poetry at the age of seven. Mrs. Young, my piano teacher, was a perfectionist. I worked with the best talent in Canada from Karen Kain to Lynn Seymour; Martha Henry to Helen Shaver; the McGarrigle Sisters to k.d. laing; Margaret Atwood and Alice Munro; playwrights Joan MacLeod and Wendy Lill; directors Kathy Gilday and Lisa Jackson; three governors general, Jeanne Sauvé, Adrienne Clarkson, and Michaëlle Jean; two Canadian consuls general, Kim Campbell in Los Angeles and Pamela Wallin in New York; top television executives Trina McQueen and Michelle Fortin; fellow lobbyists Nicole Boisvert and Danielle Suissa; production partners Barbara Hager, Hilary Prior, Jennifer Puncher, Marie-José Raymond, Julia Sereny, and Katherine Smalley; Andra Sheffer in her several roles from the Academy to fund manager; and Sheena Macdonald, firstly at Rhombus and then at the Canadian Film Centre; at Banff a host of excellent co-workers from my conference team Carole Orr and Joni Cooper to Kerry Stauffer and Pauline Martin as well as my faithful executive assistants Kim Young and Chris Anderson; I can add Heidi Allebone, Esme Comfort, Cathy De Geer, Claire Honeyman, and on through the alphabet to Liz Smeaton and Berni Wood; and throughout all this the wise counsel and enduring friendship of Marcia McClung.

There is a similar international list of impressive women, but let me limit it to six extraordinary women: from the UK Ros Borland with whom I partnered on *Sharing Stories*; from France, my wonderful and long-time colleague Sylvie Brauns, who in turn introduced me to Orna Yarmut from Israel with whom I built CoPro in Tel Aviv until Orna's untimely death. Also, from France, broadcaster Ann Julienne who proved to be such a wise counsellor for the World Congress of Science Producers. From Australia, Tania Chambers who helped us launch our foray into international leadership training. And from Taiwan and China, brilliant former McKinsey executive Ruby Chen at CNEX with whom I now work closely on my training and pitching ventures in China and Taiwan. What good fortune to have worked and spent time in such company.

It would be remiss if I did not thank Michael Allder (who commissioned Darwin's Brave New World while at CBC and who directed Listening To Orcas) and his partner, author and screenwriter Gail Gallant for their support and friendship through my many ups and down in the past dozen years, coupled with their enthusiastic and active support in the writing of this book.

I would aslo like to thank for his inspirational support my publisher Ken Whyte and his impressive team at Sutherland House, in particular Leah Ciani and Jamie Weinman.

This is truly a collaborative business. My colleagues made me look good. My deficiencies are mine alone.

Ilustrations:

Her Excellency the Right Honourable Michaëlle Jean, 27th Governor General of Canada (2005–2010) presented the Member insignia of the Order of Canada to W. Paterson Ferns, C.M., during an investiture ceremony held at Rideau Hall, in Ottawa, on October 6, 2006.

Photo credit: MCpl Issa Paré, Rideau Hall © OSGG, 2006
© His Majesty the King in Right of Canada represented by the OSGG, 2006. Reproduced with permission of the Office of the Secretary to the Governor General, 2025.

The Wars - Photo Credit: Shin Sugino

INDEX: PEOPLE, PROGRAMS AND FILMS